CODES, CIPHERS, AND SECRET LANGUAGES

FRED B. WRIXON

HARRAP

LONDON

100515 To my family

Permission was granted for use of the following:

Ardois System from *Proceedings of United States Naval Institute.*

Excerpts from *Book of Pidgin English* by John J. Murphy. Reprinted by AMS Press, Inc., New York.

Cyrillic Alphabet Chart and L'Epee Alphabet from *The Encyclopedia Americana,* © 1986 by Grolier, Inc., Danbury, Connecticut.

Howard H. Peckham's British Secret Writing Facts by the William L. Clements Library, University of Michigan.

Indian Sign Language by William Tomkins, Dover Publications, Inc., New York, 1968.

Myer/Wigwag Facts by the United States Army Military History Institute.

Scout Trail Signs by the Boy Scouts of America.

Semaphore Chart from *The Bluejackets' Manual,* 20th edition, edited by Bill Bearden. Copyright © 1978, United States Naval Institute, Annapolis, Maryland.

Copyright © 1989 by Fred B. Wrixon

Published in Great Britain 1989 by Harrap Books Ltd.,
19–23 Ludgate Hill, London EC4M 7PD, by arrangement with
Crown Publishers, Inc.

Manufactured in the United States of America

Wrixon, Fred B.
  Codes, ciphers, and secret languages.

  Bibliography: p.
  1. Ciphers—History. 2. Cryptography—History.
I. Title.
Z103.W77 1989   652'.8   87-32580
ISBN 0-245-54880-7

Book design by Cynthia Dunne

h g f e d c b a

CONTENTS

INTRODUCTION

↢↢↢↢

The words *codes, ciphers,* and *secret languages* often conjure images of spies, fog-shrouded rendezvous, and threats to national security. Certainly this has been true through the centuries as wars, boundaries, and crowned heads have been directly affected by well-prepared communications. The disguised contents found in both hidden messages and signal methods have turned losing skirmishes into winning battles and have diminished the power of royalty at the height of their glory. From the times of courageous but ill-fated cavalry charges to the present debates over verifying nuclear weapons, the use or misuse of codes, ciphers, and secret languages has proven to be crucial.

This book provides numerous examples of puzzles that have confounded experts from the alchemists of yore to modern computer cryptologists. *Codes, Ciphers, and Secret Languages* also lets you return to the time when powerful Sparta was rescued by ingenious commanders who saved their people by the twist of a scepter and discover how privateers and their modern navy counterparts sent cryptic words on the high seas. Or perhaps your interests are inclined toward the type of court intrigue associated with rulers such as Elizabeth I of England and Mary, Queen of Scots; poorly disguised messages played a large part in deciding the outcome of their bitter rivalry. Centuries later, the well-concealed secret language of the Navajo Indians contributed much to America's victory in World War II.

The following chapters contain many examples of the secret worlds of codes, ciphers, and secret languages. After each section you can enter the mysterious cryptanalyst's chambers for a real test of wits. Here you can make discoveries by inserting a priming key, exchanging code and symbol, twisting a cipher disk, or using other cryptographic secrets. Whatever system you choose, the myriad pleasures of secret communication await you.

ACKNOWLEDGMENTS

I wish to express my appreciation for the prompt and efficient services provided by the staff members of the following: Army Communications–Electronics Museum, Fort Monmouth, New Jersey; Naval Historical Center, Washington, D.C.; Ohio County Public Library, Wheeling, West Virginia; *The Encyclopedia Americana* (Grolier, Inc., Danbury, Connecticut; U.S. Army Military History Institute, Carlisle Barracks, Pennsylvania.

I.

BEGINNINGS

1

FOUNDATIONS

⟨⟨⟨⟨

News reports and headlines are often dominated by accounts of espionage, spy rings, and suspected traitors. Sharing the newsprint and camera lights are reports of arms-control debates, weapons like the stealth bomber, and futuristic space research. These subjects are connected to each other in terms of military and national security interests. Sometimes such issues seem vague and too complex for most of us to understand, but they fascinate us nonetheless.

Cinematic and real-life spies are expected to send concealed messages. Diplomats have special phrases for embassy and personal use. Childhood friends and fraternal organizations alike use particular terms for initiations, ceremonial programs, and ongoing brotherhood. Women's clubs and charitable organizations often have passwords as a part of their traditions or just for amusement. Thus, in one way or another most people are familiar with such methods. Concealment, ritualistic oaths, and linguistic variations all involve codes, ciphers, and secret languages. Each of the words in this book's title is an entity unto itself. *Codes* and *ciphers* can be broadly defined as the means by which messages are hidden, or masked, by a sender so that only a designated recipient can interpret the correspondence. The concealment methods are intended to deny access by a third party (i.e., "the enemy") to the contents. Yet though the terms *ciphers* and *codes* are often used interchangeably, each has distinctive properties. A full understanding of these terms requires knowledge of their similarities and differences.

The same is true for the terms *secret writing* and *secret language,* which are sometimes erroneously applied both to codes and ciphers and to each other. In certain eras, the distinctions between these words were not clear. For our purposes, however, these terms will be given separate functions. The term *secret writing* will be used to refer in a generalized way to codes and ciphers. *Secret language* will refer to such things as: alphabets, argot, jargon, sign language, and slang.

In addition to the various types of communication described above, we will also be looking at various *means* of communication: written and verbal terms are only a subset. For example, within the realm of military signaling we find: persons holding and/or waving objects; mounted or moving shapes; free-burning or fixed illumination; and mechanical and electrical devices, to name some basic styles. A complete overview of signaling methods would have to include everything from the smoke signals of Alexander the Great to today's world of technological wizardry.

The following definitions have been combined from several sources. They are in alphabetical order and are intended to serve as a convenient in-chapter glossary.

CRYPTOLOGY VOCABULARY

Cipher (Arabic: *sifr,* nothing)—A means of concealing a message. The letters of the message are substituted or transposed for other letters, letter pairs *(bigrams* or *digraph),* and sometimes for many letters *(polygrams).*

Cipher Alphabet—A list of letters or other equivalent forms that enable the cipher creator to transform a message into a secret configuration.

Ciphertext—The original words of a message after they have been transformed into cipher forms.

Cleartext—A communication that is sent without encoding or enciphering. It is also referred to as *in clear.*

Code (French: *codex,* tree trunk, writing tablet)—A method of concealment that may use words, numbers, or syllables to replace the original words and/or phrases of a message. One specific way that codes differ from ciphers is by the substitution of whole words as contrasted with the letters that are substituted or transposed in ciphers.

Codetext—The original words of a message after they have been transformed into code forms.

Cryptanalyst—One who deciphers or decodes without possessing the concealment method being used. He or she is a third party who applies various means to reveal the contents of others' secret messages.

Cryptogram (Greek: *kryptos,* hidden + *gram,* written or drawn)—The complete, altered, secret message that is sent.

Cryptology (Greek: *kryptos,* hidden + *logos,* word)—The science that includes making messages secret *(cryptography)* and the solving of those messages by those meant to have them *(deciphering* and *decoding)* or by third parties, the "opponents", who are not meant to have them.

Decipher—To reverse a cipher concealment by using the particular method needed to reveal the true contents.

Decode—To reverse a code concealment by using the particular method needed to reveal the actual message.

Digraph—An encipherment in which the *plaintext* is written using letter pairs.

Frequency Tables—Lists used by cryptanalysts that show frequency of letters, letter pairs, syllables, and words in various languages. These tables help the analyst find similar patterns.

Ideograph—A graphic (written) symbol of an idea or object that does not represent the sounds that make its name but rather an idea.

Key—A term that identifies the proper arrangement of a cipher alphabet, the set-up of letters in a transposition, the disk alignments of a cipher machine, and so forth. The terms *key phrase, key word,* and *key number* indicate the use of a particular phrase, word, or number, respectively, as a key. (Obviously, the sender and receiver must use the same key.)

Monalphabetic—Using a single cipher alphabet to create a ciphered communication.

Nomenclator—A codelike system used between 1400 and 1850. It often consisted of a cipher alphabet and a coded group of words, names, and syllables.

Null—A letter or symbol in a cipher alphabet chosen to mean nothing. *Nulls* may be used to complete a particular pattern of letters or numbers that would otherwise be uneven (as in making pairs). They can also be used to confuse a potential cryptanalyst because they don't equate with any other letter, pattern, etc.

Plaintext—The recognizable material that appears after the successful completion of decoding, deciphering, or cryptanalysis. It is also the original message placed in the cipher or code maze.

Polyalphabetic—Using more than one cipher alphabet to create a ciphered communication.

Steganography—A method that masks a communication by such means as disguising it with invisible ink or hiding it in a microdot. Steganography conceals an entire message rather than altering its contents.

Substitution—A system of cryptography whereby the letters of a message are replaced by other figures, numbers, or letters.

Transposition—A system of cryptography whereby the letters of a message are rearranged. Generally, it is a less complicated method than *substitution*.

With these definitions in mind, let's consider some of the foundation principles of these methods.

While codes were the prime choice for masking communications in the past, ciphers have been predominant since the early 1900s. Ciphers have proved to be better adapted than codes in the modern electronic age because of the easy application of their two main forms: transposition and substitution.

A cipher is created with groups of letters. The letters vary with the given message. Nevertheless all practical cipher systems should have the following: a key; set rules of procedure; and a clear understanding of the methods to be used between the sender and the receiver.

The key should be varied for security purposes. Such a word or phrase used too often can be spotted by a wise cryptanalyst. However, a key should not be altered during any one given information exchange. It determines the procedure to be followed, the structure of the created cipher, and the pattern of decipherment by the recipient (who should have a matching key for every planned exchange).

Transposition ciphers have rearranged letters and are often associated with a kind of geometric design. A typical example of this type is the *columnar cipher.*

A columnar cipher often has its plaintext letters placed in a rectangle. The words (letters) follow a horizontal pattern from left to right and top to bottom. A key determines the order in which the letters are taken from the columns. In the following example the letters will be aligned as ciphertext in four-letter groups.

The key is numerical and is formed by a simple process. Suppose our key word is diplomat. Its letters are simply numbered according to their position in the standard English alphabet (1 to 26). Thus, d = 4, i = 9, p = 16, l = 12, o = 15, m = 13, a = 1, t = 20. This key word and its corresponding numbers are placed above the plaintext message, microfilm will be arriving by courier, which is itself placed in a rectangle:

d	i	p	l	o	m	a	t
4	9	16	12	15	13	1	20
m	i	c	r	o	f	i	l
m	w	i	l	l	b	e	a
r	r	i	v	i	n	g	b
y	c	o	u	r	i	e	r

Next we look at a, the first alphabet letter, and the column beneath it, with the letters, i e g e. This becomes the first line of ciphertext. The next letter in alphabetical order, d (4), has the column letters, m m r y. Follow this same procedure to complete the ciphered message:

iege mmry iwrc rlvu fbni olir ciio labr

When the recipient gets this message, he or she would have the correct key word (diplomat) to decipher the letters. The recipient prepares a rectangle, or other preset geometric figure, with the necessary number of spaces for letters (based on the length of the key and the message). The text is written in each column, down the columns in alignment with the numerical key:

d	i	p	l	o	m	a	t
4	9	16	12	15	13	1	20
m	i		r				i
m	w		l				e
r	r		v				g
y	c		u				e

By the time the first four columns are filled in, the original facts about the arrival of the microfilm are beginning to appear. The recipient knows to read the letters in a normal left-to-right manner in order to recover the full message.

A standard example of a *substitution cipher* is a double parallel alphabet, which also evolves from a key word. In the following example, there is a special requirement: the word must have at least seven letters. The key word is followed by the remaining letters of the alphabet not found in the key itself. Underneath these letters, we write the regular alphabet (a to z). For the key word, use ciphers.

```
c i p h e r s a b d f g j k l m n o q t u v w x y z
─────────────────────────────────────────────────
a b c d e f g h i j k l m n o p q r s t u v w x y z
```

Let's suppose it is necessary to send a communication saying, go fast. First find g in the standard alphabet. It is positioned beneath s which thus becomes the cipher letter for g. The letter o is found below l, which is its concealed equivalent. When this pattern of substitutions is completed, the letters form: sl rc qt. Since this example was in a general stage, t happened to align with itself. Even a slight shift or alteration would change that and create many other possibilities.

The recipient also has the key word, ciphers. He or she then sets up a parallel arrangement in the same manner. The next step is simply to look for the letters in reverse. Thus s = g, l = o, etc. to reveal go fast once more.

The configurations described above are monalphabetic, with plain and cipher equivalents being single letters. It is possible to introduce another level of difficulty with what are called *multiliteral* systems. In such systems, two or more figures, digits, or letters equate with the cipher. They are produced from diagrams like these:

A

	g	r	e	e	n
b	a	b	c	d	e
r	f	g	h	i	j
o	k	l	m	n	o
w	p	q	r	s	t
n	u	v	w	x	yz

B

	0	1	2	3	4	5	6	7	8	9
0	d	o	c	u	m	e	n	t	a	b
1	f	g	h	i	j	k	l	p	q	r
2	s	v	w	x	y	z	*	*	*	*

Notice in matrix *A* that the infrequently used letters y and z are combined in one corner or *cell* to create a figure with even rows. In matrix *B*, a key word is followed by the remaining alphabet letters, and asterisks are used as *nulls* (see definitions on page 6) to complete the diagram.

To encipher with either of these matrices, one begins by choosing the letters at the *coordinates* (meeting point) of the column and row where the plaintext letter appears. Let's assume that we wish to conceal the letter i. In matrix *A* the letters that meet at the row and column point of i are r and e. In matrix *B*, the numbers thus meeting on a line of intersection with i's position are l and 3. Continuing in this fashion, the word intercept could be masked with dual letters or numbers as follows:

	i	n	t	e	r	c	e	p	t
TYPE A	re	oe	wn	bn	we	be	bn	wg	wn
TYPE B	13	06	07	05	19	02	05	17	07

Codes are the other primary concealment method. A code is a special form of substitution. It consists of such combinations as figures, symbols, groups of numbers/letters, phrases, etc. that act as equivalents in replacing the plaintext words. A code for country capitals might look something like this:

PLAINTEXT	CODE
Washington, D.C.	200
London	castle
Madrid	# # #
Paris	gourmet
Rome	hills
Oslo	+ + + +
Vienna	100-lakes

Whereas ciphers use plaintext elements of regular length, codes operate with letter and number groups of varying length. Another difference between the two is that codes usually use entire words or number sets while ciphers frequently divide syllables or split numbers. Codes usually require a *code book* for encoding (making) and decoding them. Such collections are necessary because corresponding persons using codes need to be certain both of the method of substitution and the definitions of the terms.

While code books are often depicted as the object of military espionage, they are also used in industrial spying. In today's global competition for technology, businesses have had to conceal their national and international correspondence, particularly in Western nations where there is freer access to information than is available elsewhere. Industries also use codes for practical and economic reasons. Since codes can represent groups of words, one code element can replace a sentence, phrase, or list of terms in an otherwise costly telegram or computer/ phone transmission.

Codes can be constructed on a one-part or two-part basis. The former are called *alphabetical* or *numerical* codes, while the latter are known as *randomized* codes. As the names imply, one-part codes are set up in numerical or alphabetical order. These serve both encoding and decoding purposes. Two-part codes have plaintext in alphabetical and numerical order, but their coded equivalents are random. Chance decides the matching factors for two-part codes. Unlike the one-part style, these can only be used for code making. For decoding, a separate list is needed to compensate for the chance factor.

Codes may also be subjected to an enciphering process. This can be done by using transposition or substitution methods with already encoded material. Some businesses have words that are difficult to conceal with other terms alone. Sometimes the use of one phrase unique to a business may actually indicate clues to the facts being hidden. Under these circumstances, enciphering methods are added for more security.

Such protection efforts are necessary and must be constantly updated due to the efforts of cryptanalysts, those who find ways to break or "pry loose" the numerical or verbal seals in which others encase their communications. Just as with the cipher/code makers, the cipher/code breakers can be found in science, industry, diplomacy, and espionage.

Cryptanalysis began with the same foundations as did code/cipher creating. Eventually, after much trial and error, more efficient methods developed. Like the creators, the breakers require perseverance, intuition, and imagination. These abilities are applied in a series of steps that could include:

1. Knowledge of the situation (e.g., war, spies, or ambassadors) for which the particular masking system has been created. For instance, if the assignment were to solve diplomatic exchanges, one wouldn't spend much time looking for references to the plans of an agricultural conglomerate.

2. Detailed study and arrangement of the material in order to reveal nonrandom facts. Nonrandom data strongly indicate such factors as a series of letters or numbers that repeat in certain identifiable ways.

3. Applying known charts of number and letter frequency according to the particular languages, signal devices, embassies, and so forth with which the message is associated.

4. Linking the repetitions to the proper systems. Cryptanalysts know the tricks of substitution and transposition, but for the sake of

time, they must use all of their tools of deductive and inductive reasoning to determine which of the dozens of existing styles have been used to mask the puzzle before them.

There are, of course, many other methods of cryptanalysis. What is important to remember is that the code/cipher breaker can apply his or her own methods. Over the centuries successes and failures, using everything from parchment to modern technical devices, have taught valued lessons. One of the most important of these lessons involves the concept of *frequency,* as mentioned in the preceding list. Let's take a closer look at its potential uses.

The contrived word *etaonrish* is a favorite of cryptanalysts working with the English language. This "word" is actually made up of those letters most often used in English. The precise ordering of these letters varies with different usage tabulations, but the letter e tops almost every list of any size and is usually followed by these other eight letters: t, a, o, n, r, i, s, and h.

A second frequency pattern exists for digraphs (letter pairs). Some of the most common pairs are: en, re, nt, th, and an. Of course, single-letter frequency is, in part, a function of digraph frequency. The same holds true for trigraphs (three-letter combinations) such as ent, ion, and tio. These groups appear frequently because of the word-formation patterns of the English language.

Along with frequency charts, a cipher solver applies tables of a language's words listed by length, rhyming sequences, popular phrases, and even jargon or slang. Repetition is a primary factor in almost all of these particular types of speech.

Using some or all of this supportive knowledge, a cryptanalyst begins to attack a cipher's defenses. Knowing that the number of plain and masked elements of a transposition is often exact in number, he or she can gain a grip with a letter count. Frequency lists are particularly helpful when there is a pattern of repetitive letters. For example, zz or 11 may very well be ee or oo. This is the awkward but necessary way in which the first wedges can be driven into a cipher. A suspected transposition can be further "assaulted" by placing the numbers or letters in the various types of geometric designs mentioned earlier. However, more letters don't necessarily mean one should try a parallelogram instead of a rectangle, or a triangle instead of a square. One or all of these configurations might be applicable.

A substitution can be best analyzed by frequency when it is mono-alphabetic. Because substitutions often involve multiple alphabets, however, these must be reduced to simpler forms. Frequency tables, word lists, jargon, and the like can be directed in stages, each aimed at finding the possible links between the ciphertext letters and the ciphered alphabets to which they belong. Geometric forms are not much of a help here, as substitutions don't conform well to their shapes. Rather, substitutions can "tip the dominoes" of a complicated alphabet to reveal its base parts.

For code solving, some of the previously mentioned techniques are helpful. Yet perhaps more important is the solver's basic understanding of the language(s) involved. Knowledge of jargon and popular slogans are sometimes particularly helpful because of the arbitrary and contrived terms of a code. Intuition, gained from experience, can also have an important role.

The background of cipher, code, and secret language developments will unfold in the following chapters.

We'll be finding out about methods with names like *polyalphabet, grille, auto key, square, route,* and *one-time pad,* to name but a few. Whatever the name or method of the missive or sending mechanism, keep the definitions in this chapter in mind and build carefully upon their foundation.

2

YEARS OF YORE

⟨⟨⟨⟨ •

Egypt, an advanced early civilization, was the first in recorded history to use aspects of cryptology in writing. Early Egyptian hieroglyphics contained some figures that were somewhat altered from their original form. This was apparently done simply to give the symbols an extra flair, or increased status. Though not a code or cipher by any means, this change did involve a basic principle of cryptology, namely, that of transforming writing.

As the Egyptian civilization expanded, hieroglyphics became more involved. Symbols, pictographic representations, and pronunciation became intertwined. With the increasing numbers of carvings on special edifices, the once curious populace became disinterested. Egyptologists and others theorize that the official scribes then modified some figures still further in an attempt to regain the public's interest through curiosity.

This writing was used primarily to describe religious texts and rituals. In a desire to protect these texts and impart their teachings with added respect, priests had scribes make still more changes. When special figures were created for these specific purposes, *secrecy,* another central principle of cryptology, became involved. The religious hierarchy took advantage of its powers of "translation" for the increasingly less informed, and thus more dependent, people.

Still, while the Nile's masters had indirectly developed two standard cryptological principles, there are no clear records indicating that they used these methods to conceal diplomatic, commercial, or military gain as a national policy.

Looking toward the east and the advanced Chinese civilization, one finds their style of ideographic writing is obvious, but their figures seemingly did not lend themselves well to secrecy. Altering parts of any one or several of the forms did not accomplish true concealment. Thus, couriers generally carried reports or commands by word of mouth.

By A.D. 1000 they were placing very important messages on silk paper. Then they rolled the missive into a ball and covered it with wax. This could be viewed as an early attempt at a type of *steganography,* a concealment method that utilizes special materials.

At this same time a second well-established people who used more detailed hidden communications were natives of India. The rulers of this multifaceted region had personal watchers who made up a kind of internal spy network. Their methods included: phonetic substitutions (consonants and vowels switched), reversed letters aligned with one another, and styles of writing that were placed at odd angles.

Two curious versions of secrets and the means of conveying them were found in a system of special gestures and an erotic book. The former was a clever use of the fingers adapted by the hearing- and speech-impaired. Most versions of this method equated digits with consonants and the joints with vowels. Some also assigned meanings to the spaces between the fingers. This type of very primitive sign language continued into more modern times in the form of signals used by beggars and money lenders.

Regarding the latter work, knowledge of concealed writing is included as one of the more than sixty skills to be mastered by women in the *Kāma-sūtra.* This text by an Indian named Vātsyāyana is a compilation of sexual material still used by modern-day sex therapists. Vātsyāyana's collection indicates an awareness of obscuring methods in India on a broader scale than existed at that time in China.

Other civilizations were prospering in Mesopotamia as well as in the eastern Mediterranean areas settled by the Jewish people. *Cuneiform* writing was the prime means of recording the daily lives of Mesopotamian empire builders like the Babylonians, Assyrians, and Chaldeans. Actually, as early as 1500 B.C. a cuneiform tablet held a carefully guarded "recipe" for a pottery-glazing material. The mixture of cuneiform figures defining the proper ingredients was purposely jumbled. Thus, it might rightly be called the first known attempt of hiding words.

Here are some examples of (A) hieroglyphic and (B) cuneiform writing:

(A)　　woman　　　house　　　man

(B) woman house man

The Mediterranean shores provide somewhat clearer cryptological examples. Though also partially obscured by time, this region had many traditions of verbal and written records. Because of the multitude of events, people, and locales described in the Bible, we also know about a man who can be called the world's "first cryptanalyst."

The Biblical account of Daniel is familiar to many. Daniel was made a captive when the Babylonian Nebuchadnezzar conquered Palestine in 605 B.C. Being a young prisoner, Daniel grew up in Babylon as Nebuchadnezzar became king. A wise young man credited with the ability to intrepret dreams, Daniel became influential with a succession of rulers including Neriglissar, Labash-Marduk, and Nabonidas. Daniel rose to prominence in the social order and understood every aspect of Babylon's culture. Yet he kept his faith and moral principles amidst idolatry and a kingdom becoming badly encumbered with its own lavish excesses. Thus was the stage set for Daniel's ultimate prophecy.

By 534 B.C. Belshazzar, son of Nabonidas, ruled a nation weakened by the corruption of unchecked power and the symptoms of decadence. Belshazzar had lost the loyalty of the people whose ancestors had fought bravely and well for Nebuchadnezzar. Daniel, now an old but still brilliant man, had been in attendance at one of the king's feasts. In the midst of the revelry came the stark archetype of all predictions of doom; *Mene Mene Tekel Upharsin* was seen as the handwriting on the wall (Daniel 5:5-28).

From a cryptological point of view these words were not particularly secretive in a strictly linguistic sense. In fact, it can be argued that transformation in a literal sense was absent. Yet this only heightens our fascination with the account.

The words *mene, tekel,* and *upharsin* had equivalents in Aramaic names for money. A *mina* ("mene") was a coin defined by some dictionaries as 1/60 of a *talent* (approximately 58 pounds). Thus, a *mina* weighed approximately one pound. A *tekel* ("tekel") was quite similar to the Aramaic shekel and was 1/60 of a *mina*. A *peres* ("upharsin") was worth half a *mina*. These monetary types give credence to the belief that the words symbolized the financial separation of Babylon and its wealth (empire). This made Daniel a cryptanalyst of a phrase that was not apparently masked. Or did it? Why were Belshazzar and his soothsayers unable to discern these relatively familiar words?

It should be remembered that the Bible credits Daniel's prescience to the inspiration of God. Belshazzar and the others would naturally have been stunned by the appearance of the words. In a nation of idol worshipping and mysticism, such an occurrence would have been quite a shock. Perhaps they were dumbfounded, unable to "put two and two together." Even more likely is the possibility that God may have confused the others while he gave foreknowledge to Daniel. The wise Jewish captive interpreted the phrase this way: *Mene*—God hath numbered thy kingdom, and finished it. *Tekel*—Thou art weighed in the balances and art found wanting. *Peres*—Thy kingdom is divided and given to the Medes and Persians. (*Peres* in Aramaic was identical with upharsin.)

According to the Bible, Belshazzar was slain that very night. Darius, a Medean, assumed control. Not long thereafter, a powerful Persian commander, Cyrus, conquered the entire Babylonian empire. With his conquest, once mighty Babylon was no more; Daniel's prediction had been correct.

Cyrus and other Persian leaders were to have their days of glory. Then they too fell into the self-created trap of overextending themselves. When they tried to spread the boundaries of their empire toward the Aegean Sea, they ran into staunch resistance from the Greek city-states, especially Sparta and Athens. This Persian-Greek conflict provided more detailed facts about how advanced civilizations concealed messages and transmitted signals. Accounts of such methods became possible because the traditions of oral story telling had evolved into written record keeping.

Actually, as early as the fourth century B.C., the Persians had a full-fledged messenger service that traversed the realm of King Darius. He sent word to friends, warnings to enemies, and notices to tax collectors alike over these routes. A very credible predecessor to the Pony Express, this system used fresh mounts and couriers located at sites not more than a day's riding distance apart. During times of impending conflict, these same swift horsemen quickly roused the troops into action. This was done on a grand scale when another Persian leader, Xerxes I, had elaborate dreams of conquest. It was he who planned the largest invasion yet against the city-states.

The Greek historian Herodotus wrote that the warning that saved the Greeks was sent by secret means. A man named Demaratus had heard that Xerxes was on the march. Demaratus wanted to send word to the Spartans, the most war-ready people in the Aegean region. He used a makeshift concealment device created by scraping wax from two wooden tablets. Demaratus enscribed what he knew of the Persians' intentions, then replaced the wax covering. The seemingly plain tablets were passed untouched to Spartan control.

In Sparta a wise woman named Gorgo studied the tablets. The wife of the Spartan commander Leonidas, it was she who discovered the hidden facts. Her means of discovery have been shrouded by time. She has a very strong claim to being the world's first female cryptanalyst. Yet, Gorgo's achievement was bittersweet. It was her spouse, Leonidas, who loyally rushed into action with his men. They hastened by forced march to a crucial defensive position on the route of the Persian onslaught. The site was a pass called Thermopylae. Traitors and their knowledge of a hidden path led to the defeat of Leonidas and his troops. But the brave 300 held their position for three days, allowing the city-states time to prepare and enriching the honor of the Spartan warriors.

The waxed tablets were a kind of steganography. Herodotus described other versions of this device that were both practical and ingenious. He documented stories of men posing as hunters with missives concealed inside their day's catch. He also told of a plan by which the heads of slaves were shaved. Orders or replies were tatooed on the bald spots. When time restored their hair, the shaving process was repeated.

Thanks to other noted Greek historians, including Polybius and Thucydides, we know about still other concealment methods of this era. Thucydides described what is believed to be the first complete system of transferring secret information. He credits the Spartans with accomplishing this by using a device called a *skytale* (rhymes with *Italy*).

The skytale may be the oldest means used to convey secrets. A method of transposition, it was a type of staff or rod around which a message-carrying material was tightly wrapped. The substances thus applied included cloth, leather, and paper. The actual letters of the communication were written along the length of the rod. Then meaningless nulls were placed around it. (Actually, efforts to create other sensible phrases were more time consuming than protective.) Once the material was unwound, the chosen letters "blended" visually with all the others.

It was not necessary for the recipient Spartans or their allies to have an elaborate code to keep or memorize. They did need a piece of wood or metal of the same thickness as that used by the senders. Once the parchment or cloth was wound closely again, the intended letters resumed their original word forms. Here is an example of how a skytale might have looked:

Athens and the other city-states of the Greek isles also had special methods of signaling. They used illumination by fire, which was a necessary navigational aid around and through the numerous Greek shoals. From lamps and torches mounted in clear, high sites as well as from flames used to mark dangerous waters, more elaborate transmission systems developed.

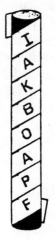

Polybius described the creation of other systems as well as one that he helped develop. A Greek known as Aeneas the Tactician compiled texts about warfare around 350–345 B.C. One of the best encoding devices used by Aeneas may be called *elemental transferral*. In those days, earth, air, water, and fire were considered the basic elements of all physical matter. Aeneas combined each of them to create a signaling apparatus.

The system consisted of torches, earthen containers, and supplies of water to send "across the air" to another such setup. Water was poured into a four-foot-deep container that had a controlled stopper or valve. On the water was placed a cork with an attached graduated rod. At various levels on the rod were war words or terms. A torch was waved to alert the next station to be ready. The receiving observers held up a torch or torches in a planned response for "ready." The lights were then shielded and the stations began a mutual signaling process. The valves of both containers were opened, permitting the water and cork to descend in each. When the graduated rod (and its corresponding term) reached the upper rim of the barrel, the sender again displayed his torch as a sign to halt the flow of water. The receivers applied their stopper, then read the words at the graduated mark on their cork float.

Though this seems quite an awkward method by modern standards, the writings of Polybius indicate that the device may have been used in actual sieges. He was so intrigued by such accounts that he applied himself to devising a signaling system of his own.

A long tradition of fire-based signals was already in existence for Polybius to study. Greek mythology had tales of torch-sent messages. Crude towers supposedly bore news, in the form of fire, of the fall of Troy from observers of that doomed city to Agamemnon's fortress at Mycenae. Herodotus had written of Greek vessels that sent flame warnings of the approach of a Persian fleet. Thus, it is logical that Polybius would also have experimented with a fire-based method.

Polybius credits the Greek philosopher Democritus with originating a method that Polybius "merely enhanced." Yet other researchers state that Polybius deserves praise not only for the signaling improvement but also for the cipher-making technique that grew from it.

The Democritus/Polybius flame system involved dividing the Greek alphabet into five parts containing five letters each. These five sections were in turn written on five tablets in normal letter-sequence order. The tablets were used in conjunction with a series of torches, optical instruments, and fences. Each station had torches, which were held to the right or left of a stand holding the tablets.

A flame raised directly above the sender's head could signify that alphabet tablet five should be used. Torches held to the left could indicate alphabet columns while flames directed to the right could represent rows. Thus, one torch in the left hand could mean column one and two torches in the right hand could signal row two. Other planned position changes of the flames indicated facts such as: wait for orders, or disregard previous instructions. The fence structures served to block one or more flames to avoid confusion in timing or position.

Apparently it was Polybius who refined the torch arrangements, and he may also have added the directional eyepiece. In the history of transmission methods, he is remembered for creating a true alphabet-based system. It was the tablet and its 5 × 5 configuration for which he is also best remembered in the annals of message disguising.

In cryptology this arrangement came to be known as the *Polybius checkerboard.* As a foundation system it provided a transferral of letters to numbers, a pattern that was relatively easy to recall, and a limited amount of figures (numbers and letters) with which to work. Here is the checkerboard with English-language letters. Note that to have five letters in a row, the infrequently needed letters *u* and *v* have been combined:

	1	2	3	4	5
1	a	b	c	d	e
2	f	g	h	i	j
3	k	l	m	n	o
4	p	q	r	s	t
5	uv	w	x	y	z

This system can be used to convert the word cover to numbers. The letter c is found at the junction of row one and column three. Thus c represented by numbers is 13.

LETTER	ROW	COLUMN
c	1	3
o	3	5
v	5	1
e	1	5
r	4	3

The person receiving the numbers 13, 35, 51, 15, and 43 would use an identical checkerboard to locate the letters. Once he or she found the letters at the converging points of the numbers, the word cover would be revealed.

Julius Caesar is a man who affected history in a number of well-documented ways including his style of hidden writing; most people are not aware that he communicated with ciphers. While he was building the Roman Empire in Gaul, he communicated with a substitution type that still bears his name today.

In the Caesar cipher the plaintext letters were substituted for letters three steps along a natural alphabet progression. Thus, if Caesar had been using English, f would have aligned with i. Continuing with all the letters, this is his cipher:

a	b	c	d	e	f	g	h	i	j	k	l	m	n	o	p	q	r	s	t	u	v	w	x	y	z
d	e	f	g	h	i	j	k	l	m	n	o	p	q	r	s	t	u	v	w	x	y	z	a	b	c

Julius Caesar lived in the era of Rome's ascent to glory. But like other nations before her, Rome entered stages of decadence and decline. When the Roman Empire finally crumbled, chaos reigned. The fragile lights of education as well as cryptology were nearly extinguished when the Dark Ages swept over much of the known world.

3

REBIRTH

←/←/←/←

T he revival of literature, art, and learning that began in fourteenth-century Italy is known as the Renaissance. After the suffering and violence of the preceding centuries, this time of rediscovery did indeed seem like a rebirth.

Some of the same scholars and cloistered monks who nurtured the fragile seeds of knowledge through those years can be credited with preserving important elements of secret writing, too. Ancient ciphers as well as several solutions were among a number of the delicate texts and scrolls protected by the learned ones.

The revival of cryptology in Europe also owes some of its impetus to the growing interest in occult writings and practices. The Dark Ages had given rise to any number of superstitions regarding the powers of mysticism. To escape their earthly woes, people had sought relief through charms, incantations, and symbols of good fortune. They longed to hear words of wisdom and predictions of better days from wizards and soothsayers alike.

Among the many images and representations of prophecy, the signs of the zodiac had widespread influence. The zodiac was very important to a group of pseudoscientists called alchemists. They dabbled in a number of experiments including a search for what they called the philosopher's stone. They wanted to use it to turn base metals into gold. Because alchemists were often accused of practicing sorcery, they frequently tried to conceal their writing with crude word substitutions.

The following chart illustrates how zodiac signs and letters could be matched.

Advances in cryptology were definitely hindered by its close association with mysticism. In the presence of the expansion of religion, especially Catholicism, secret writing was at first banned, and then outlawed in many places. Yet devout people actually helped keep cryptology alive because hidden missives proved to be both necessary and practical for them. Eventually the Catholic hierarchy also found uses for concealing their correspondence amidst interchurch disputes and confrontations with powerful royalty and nobles.

Divisions among religious groups helped lead to the creation of some basic codes with name changes, abbreviations, and some replacements of names with jargon. The dispute between the Guelphs and Ghibellines as well as the Great Schism were two examples during the 1300s.

The Guelphs, a pro-Pope faction, were in conflict with the Ghibellines of Italy, who supported the Holy Roman Emperor. Their problems were rooted in policies and mixed loyalties between temporal and Vatican rule. Similar divisions occurred during the Great Schism. In that controversy, anti-Pope factions set up a church separate from Rome in Avignon, France. Soon two Popes were trying to lead their quarreling followers. The use of codes increased as more secrecy was needed. These messages formed the basis of what was to become known as the *nomenclator* (Latin: *nomen,* name + *calator,* caller).

Nomenclators came to be the principle masking system during the next four centuries. Originally lists of names, nomenclators eventually combined the name/word equivalents of codes and the substitution aspect of ciphers. This would seem to be a repetition of encoding methods already in use in the eastern Mediterranean. Yet apparently the development of the European nomenclator and other methods was not clearly linked to particular advances elsewhere.

Noted cryptologist-historian David Kahn advances similar beliefs in his book *The Codebreakers.* Kahn maintains that Europe had its own reasons for developing codes and ciphers. The very nature of the previously mentioned conflicts and power rivalries would logically have made secrecy imperative. In addition to these stimuli for creating and removing word disguises, a number of talented individuals existed who turned their minds to creating better methods.

Like the Renaissance as a whole, cryptological advances of this period owed a great debt to Italian literature, art, and culture. It was the rivalries among the city-states of Italy that also gave rise to increased needs for secrecy. The leaders of Venice were so concerned about maintaining their security that they began to employ people to read the mail intended for other cities' ambassadors. The residents of Florence, Genoa, and Naples were soon doing the same with their own trained secretaries. This led to official sanction of what the French called the *Cabinet Noir,* or Black Chamber.

One of the earliest examples of this postal surveillance occurred in Venice in the Doge's Palace. There in a special office, or chamber, three paid cryptanalysts studied everything from the mail of important merchant families to the dispatches of ambassadors. The secretaries' discoveries enabled the leaders of Venice to plan successful military and economic strategies for decades. Such chambers became a standard aspect of court influence and intrigue.

Florence gave the world an archetypal "Renaissance man" and no-menclator-breaker named Leon Alberti. Born in 1404 Alberti was a musician, athlete, artist, and architect. He designed the famous Pitti Palace and the original Trevi Fountain. Alberti also wrote poetry, fables, and an influential treatise on architecture. It is not surprising that such a multitalented individual knew something about secret writing. Indeed, Alberti earned the title of "father of western cryptology."

Alberti gained this acclaim first by solving codes and then by uncovering the rapidly developing types called ciphers. His writing about letter frequencies and patterns is considered the first such compilation in the West. His work was particularly important because he compared Italian and Latin words in his studies. Not satisfied with his efforts, he next gave code/cipher making a two-part boost.

Alberti made a cipher disk from copper plates. On two copper circles, one large and one small, he randomly placed letters and numbers. Plaintext letters could then be matched with numbers, and ciphertexts could be made in surprisingly varied ways for those days. By mutual agreement, the correspondents would know how to align the circles and at what point in the missive the circles might be changed. This then created the possibility of prearranged multiple alphabets and meanings. Thus, the disk was in effect the original polyalphabetic cipher:

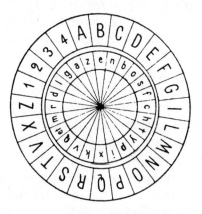

Alberti's disk also incorporated his third major contribution to cryptology. With the numbers 1 to 4 on the outer circle, he formulated a system using groups of numbers such as 11, 222, 3333, etc. in two- to four-digit combinations. By substituting numbers for letters in the optional circle turns, he had created enciphered code. Although Alberti's cryptological achievements are recognized today, they proved to be too far ahead of their time even for most others concerned with cryptology. He was a pioneer and prophet but did not become a leader. The times and situations among kings and rulers were not yet ready for a man of his vision.

The next major development in the field came from Germany. In 1462, in a town named Trittenheim, Johannes Trithemius was born. Though not the equal of the multitalented Alberti, Trithemius made contributions that were both helpful and detrimental and thus worthy of consideration.

A skilled writer, Trithemius contributed to polyalphabetic advancements by being the first to arrange such groupings in the form of a *tabula recta,* or square table. Here are some examples of one of his code lists (A) and part of the *tabula recta* (B):

(A)	A	Jesus	Eternal
	B	God	Perpetual
	C	Savior	Infinite
	D	King	Angelic
	E	Pastor	Immortal
	F	Author	Enduring
	G	Redemptor	Incomprehensible
	H	Prince	Incorruptible
	I, J	Maker	Durable
	K	Conservator	Permanent

(B) A B C D E F G H I K L M N O P Q R S T U X Y Z W

B C D E F G H I K L M N O P Q R S T U X Y Z W A

C D E F G H I K L M N O P Q R S T U X Y Z W A B

D E F G H I K L M N O P Q R S T U X Y Z W A B C

This listing was a major step forward in that it presented all the cipher alphabets in his system for viewing at one time. Trithemius called his method a "square table" because it consisted of twenty-four alphabet letters arranged in squares containing twenty-four rows. He enciphered plaintext words by transposing their letters with those in succeeding rows, moving one place to the left each time. This procedure can rightly be called the original *progressive key,* whereby every alphabet is used before any repetitions of those same groupings occur.

While developing such codes or cipher tables, Trithemius also wrote bibliographies of theological works and histories. Such important works gave credence to his writing about cryptology. Still, his scholarly writings did not entirely dispel the shadows already lurking in his background. His reputation was being sullied by a book he had published in 1499 entitled *Steganographia* (Greek for "covered writing").

This book, which was prepared in segments, revealed Trithemius's virtual obsession with matters of the occult. Along with giving names to supposedly wise spirits and descriptions of conveying words with the mind, he tried to explain the arcane teachings of a purported Egyptian priest named Hermes Trismegistus. In spite of his reputation as a writer, Trithemius's unguarded statements about the wondrous secrets of his text cast a pall over first his other works and then his life. Rumors spread that he was delving into forbidden practices and consorting with devil worshippers. Eventually he was labeled a publicity-seeking conjuror. Forced to leave his favorite abbey sanctuary, he passed away in relative obscurity in 1516.

The legacy of Trithemius can be found in polyalphabet variations, tables, and the first printed book on cryptology, *Polygraphia*. Published posthumously by his friends, its practical contents restored some luster to his reputation.

The next stage in the advancement of cryptology was made by Giovan Belaso. He was an Italian who worked in the service of a cardinal for a time. His sole but important contribution to cipher/code making was a booklet published in 1553. In it he suggested the application of a countersign, or key, for polyalphabetic methods. This key, consisting of words that were easy to recall, was placed above the message to be sent. The key letter matched with the plaintext letter signified the particular alphabet group to be used:

KEY:	I D E A S	W I N	T H E	M I N D S
PLAIN:	b r e a d	g a i	n s h	e a r t s

Key I and plain text b were aligned on a full alphabet table. Then b was enciphered by the I alphabet from the table, r by the D alphabet, and so forth. This was a "key" step forward because it broadened the choices from the few elemental systems previously used. Belaso's method also enabled keys to be replaced quickly in case of theft or loss, an advantage that contributed to its rapid acceptance, and that represented another strong block in the edifice of cryptology.

Regarding the use of alphabets, it should be remembered that Belaso had not moved forward from Alberti's mixed alphabets. Rather, his letters were standardized. It was another Italian, Giovanni Porta, who returned to Alberti's prescient methods and elaborated upon them.

Porta, a Neapolitan, was born in 1535. At an early age he became interested in earth science and published works about unusual fauna and flora. He increased his range of interests and knowledge of the world through association with various scholars. In these groups, magic, the occult, and secret incantations were discussed. However, Porta and his colleagues sought to separate fact from fantasy.

Porta might be called the "Neapolitan Newton" since among several endeavors he studied light refraction, astronomy, home construction, did crude but valid research on the properties of water, and wrote comedies. Much of this experimentation was gathered in his *Magia naturalis,* a collection of a score of books. This collection also reveals that he understood steganography: he described ways to make secret inks for placing on the flesh of messengers. In fact, he listed the majority of concealing and revealing devices of his day.

Porta also made two important additions to the field. The first was the *digraphic cipher,* a means by which one symbol could be exchanged for two letters. He presented this in two forms: a square table and a pair of disks (similar to Alberti's). In the table, letter pairs were replaced by a sign at the intersecting points of their columns and rows. The disks repeated the principle of "dialed" equivalents, as shown here:

As can be seen, the figures and Roman numerals are an elaboration of Alberti's disk system. They provided even more random choice and therefore increased the number of polyalphabets available.

Porta's second contribution was a new strategy for cryptanalysts. He suggested that they should seek what could be called the likely, or probable, word. When the sender, receiver, and subject of the message could be surmised, such words, and even phrases, might be assumed to be in the contents of the message.

For example, royalty are often addressed as *"her (or his) excellency."* Cardinals and bishops tend to speak about *faith, God, virtues,* or *sins.* The rising merchants of capitalism used words like *banks, treasury,* and *coin of the realm.* Since it was the business of cryptology and its agents to learn about the origination and destination of missives, such an idea was more practical than the guesswork it might first appear to be.

Rather than making one decisive breakthrough, Porta helped unify the efforts of his predecessors. He used combinations of the Belaso key, the mixed alphabet of Alberti, and the basic letter-enciphering style of Trithemius.

Porta actually had two predecessors, but their achievements were less noteworthy than his. Curiously, both of these men sought variations of the key theme, and one was as conscious of fame-seeking as Trithemius.

Girolamo Cardano was a Milanese doctor born in 1501. Every account of his life indicates that he sought a place in history. He tried to achieve this by writing furiously most of his life. He produced a number of speculative texts on such increasingly familiar themes as nature, astrology, and the human body, to name a few.

Cardano also attempted to develop a better cipher key, reasoning that if a regular key device provided concealment, one that differed with each message would be an outstanding addition. Cardano thought he had found the answer with what he called an *autokey,* a means by which the plaintext could be used to encipher itself. But what appeared to be good in theory was flawed in fact. The arrangement that Cardano set up created the possibility of multiple deciphered answers. Certainly no recipient would be pleased with this. Furthermore, the repetition of the plaintext letters in the key resulted in an uncertain first word. The receiver was left as confused as the cryptanalyst, since the original word was supposed to unravel the intended cipher tangle.

Cardano's dream of fame was not entirely fleeting, however. He invented a type of steganography that did prove useful, a tool known as the *Cardano grille.* This device could be made of parchment or metal. The grille consisted of a series of rectangular openings of different lengths and cut to the same height as the chosen style of writing. The sender placed the letters he wanted to use in the openings. Sometimes syllables and parts of words made wider cuts necessary. Once the intended correspondence was complete, the difficult task of building reasonable, innocent-looking sentences around it began. This flaw made such phrases a clue to the presence of disguised meanings. The receiver had a much easier time as long as the correct grille copy and letter-placement order were in his possession. Still, though difficult to construct, versions of the Cardano grille were being used into the 1700s. The following is an example of a message within a message:

```
R e m e m b e r    h i s t o r y ' s    l e s s o n s :
          6      2            8            9


d i v i d e d    n a t i o n s    f a l l
  4     5           3            7   l
```

As depicted here, the numbers (1 to 9) are to be read in order to create this additional truth about divided countries.

l—all; 2, 3, 4, 5—have; 6, 7, 8, 9—before

Another prominent individual who worked with key variations was a Frenchman named Blaise de Vigenère. Born near Paris in 1523, he entered diplomatic circles at a young age. He moved extensively through the power centers of Europe and met a number of leaders. These experiences piqued Vigenère's interest in cipher creations. Like Cardano, he worked with keys but was particularly intrigued by the notion of encoding with plaintext. However, the Frenchman then made an advancement with what was called a *priming key*. He presented it in his *Traicté des Chiffres* (1586).

This truly improved variation was actually a single letter, or *primer,* known to both correspondents. The primer enabled the recipient to recover the first letter of plaintext. This in turn was used to uncover the second ciphered letter, and thus a pattern of revelation continued. Vigenère had found a better method of security and eventually acquired the fame that Trithemius and Cardano had so energetically sought.

A man for whom notoriety and success seemed to have a natural affinity was the Englishman Baron Verulam, Viscount of St. Albans, better known to the world as Francis Bacon, statesman, philosopher, and essayist. Bacon also developed a simple cipher. In comparison with the other methods so far presented, it might be considered obvious and awkward. Yet, after other cryptologists sometimes jumbled but also skillfully realigned whole alphabets, look what Bacon did with just the first two letters of his own name:

A	aaaaa	G	aabba	N	abbaa	T	baaba
B	aaaab	H	aabbb	O	abbab	UV	baabb
C	aaaba	IJ	abaaa	P	abbba	W	babaa
D	aaabb	K	abaab	Q	abbbb	X	babab
E	aabaa	L	ababa	R	baaaa	Y	babba
F	aabab	M	ababb	S	baaab	Z	babbb

Among his diverse activities, Bacon held the position of Lord Chancellor for Queen Elizabeth I. The next chapter tells what transpired in England and other growing nation-states and how codes and ciphers were used. But first, it's time to put on your wizard's cap, tap your own lucky amulet, and prepare to enter a secret world, a maze of mysteries in the cryptanalyst's chamber.

C R Y P T A N A L Y S T ' S   C H A M B E R   I

QUIZ I

Can you apply the Polybius checkerboard to reach "checkmate" and reveal the famous sites behind the numbers? (Answers on page 255.)

1. 33, 11, 43, 11, 45, 23, 35, 34

2. 14, 15, 32, 41, 23, 24

3. 11, 45, 23, 15, 34, 44

4. 13, 54, 13, 32, 11, 14, 15, 44

5. 41, 11, 43, 45, 23, 15, 34, 35, 34

6. 32, 11, 13, 35, 34, 24, 11

7. 11, 13, 43, 35, 41, 35, 32, 24, 44

8. 41, 24, 43, 11, 15, 51, 44

9. 33, 45   35, 32, 54, 33, 41, 51, 44

10. 41, 15, 32, 35, 41, 35, 34, 34, 15, 44, 51, 44

QUIZ 2

If you understand the first Polybius puzzles, you won't have to consult the Oracle at Delphi to learn these historic names. Or will you have to admit, "It's all Greek to me"? (Answers on page 255.)

1. 23, 15, 43, 13, 51, 32, 15, 44

2. 41, 43, 24, 11, 33

3. 11, 22, 11, 33, 15, 33, 34, 35, 34

4. 32, 11, 35, 13, 35, 35, 34

5. 23, 15, 32, 15, 34   35, 21   45, 43, 35, 54

6. 41, 11, 43, 24, 44

7. 11, 13, 23, 24, 32, 32, 15, 44

8. 45, 43, 35, 25, 11, 34   23, 35, 43, 44, 15

9. 23, 15, 13, 45, 35, 43

10. 13, 32, 54, 45, 15, 33, 34, 15, 44, 45, 43, 11

QUIZ 3

Julius Caesar said, "Veni, vidi, vici" (I came, I saw, I conquered), among his many profound words. In this version of his cipher, d = a. Make twenty-six English-alphabet equivalents and say, "vici" when you uncover these people, places, and events of Caesar's day. Or will you say, "Avunculus!" (Uncle!)? (Answers on page 255.)

1. u x e l f r q

2. f o h r s d w u d

3. d x j x v w x v

4. j d x o

5. e u x w x v

6. s r p s h b

7. o h j l r q v

8. d q w r q b

9. f d o s x u q l d

10. l g h v r i p d u f k

QUIZ 4

Beware of more than the Ides of March. Be wary of ciphers appearing to be regular Caesar substitutions. This time a = w. Set up your alphabet accordingly and identify these names familiar to the Roman Empire. (Answers on page 255.)

1. p n e x q j a

2. d w j j e x w h

3. y k h k o o a q i

4. o a j w p a

5. d q j o

6. a i l a n k n

7. y w n p d w c a

8. w p p e h w

9. p e x a n

10. r e o e c k p d o

QUIZ 5

Amid scientific discovery, alchemy flourished for many years. Refer to the zodiac alphabet and learn these words linked with those who sought the philosopher's stone. (Answers on page 255.)

1. ♄ ☉ ♈ ♊ ♆ ♐ ♍ ♌

2. ♒ ☿ ☉ ♊

3. ♃ ♅ ☉ ♉ ♅ ♐

4. ☄ ☉ ♓ ♅ ♐

5. ♎ ♅ ♑ ♓ ♊ ♅

6. ♑ ♄ ☉ ♊ ♅ ♑

7. ♁ ☿ ♐ ♅

8. ♋ ♍ ♐ ♓ ☉ ♐

9. ♊ ♅ ☉ ♆

10. ♄ ♂ ☉ ♐ ♄ ♍ ☉ ♊

QUIZ 6

Refer to the Alberti cipher disk and its letter alignment to determine the names of these Renaissance cities. (Answers on page 255.)

1. f o y p z

2. n p y v q z y q c y p i h o

3. et o y c n o

4. f k o y z b z

5. y z i h o v

6. e z k n o h p y z

7. k o c t v

8. s h p k o y n o

9. t z b k c b

10. z et c f y p y

QUIZ 7

Apply the Alberti cipher disk once more to uncover the names of prominent Renaissance leaders. (Answers on page 255.)

1. c v z e o h h z

2. i p h p

3. k e z n p y

4. n p k q o r

5. b z f z t z

6. s o k b c y z y b

7. b o h o p y

8. n o k et z y q o v

9. t z f o h h z y

10. n b o t o b c n c

QUIZ 8

The Porta disk will help you unravel these facts related to Renaissance explorers. (Answers on page 255.)

1.   ⌖ ✳ ✳ ✳   ✳ ✛ ⊠ ▢

2.   ✳ ✛ ✜ ⊠ ✛ ╫ ✳ ▢ ✳

3.   ⌖ ✳ ⊠ ✜ ✛ ■ ⊠ ✳ ✳ ✳ ✳ ⊠

4.   ✛ ✳ ✛ ⊠ ✳ ╫ ◉ ▢ ✳

5.   ✳ ✛ ◉ ✳   ✳ ✳ ✛ ✛ ✳ ■ ✳

6.   ⌖ ✛ ⊗ ✳ ✳ ✛ ✛

7.   ✛ ✜   ⌖ ✳ ⊠ ◉ ✛ ✛ ✳ ✳ ✳ ⊠

8.   ▢ ✳ ⊖ ◉ ■ ✳ ✛ ✛ ⊠

9.   ✜ ◉ ▫ ✳ ✛

10.   ⌖ ✳ ✳ ✳ ✛ ○ ■ ✛ ✛ ▫ ✳ ✛ ✳ ✳

QUIZ 9

From the Roman numerals on the Porta disk, find the letter equivalents of words of "interest" relating to capitalism. (Answers on page 255.)

1. XVII I XIX IX XII VII XVII

2. X XIII I XII

3. IIII V XI I XII IIII

4. VI XVI V V   XVIII XVI I IIII V

5. XI V XVI III VIII I XII XVIII

6. II XIII XII IIII XVII

7. XIIII XVI XIII VI IX XVIII

8. IX XII XIX V XVII XVIII XIII XVI

9. VI IX XII I XII III IX I X

10. XI IX IIII IIII X V   III X I XVII XVII

QUIZ 10

During the time of Francis Bacon there was much interest in magic and the occult. Apply his cipher here, and—abracadabra! (Answers on page 255.)

1. babaa, abaaa, baaba, aaaba, aabbb

2. aaabb, aabaa, ababb, abbab, abbaa, baaab

3. abbba, aabaa, abbaa, baaba, aaaaa, aaaba, ababa, aabaa

4. baaab, abbab, baaaa, aaaba, aabaa, baaaa, babba

5. aabaa, baabb, abaaa, ababa   aabaa, babba, aabaa

6. babaa, aaaaa, baaaa, ababa, abbab, aaaba, abaab

7. aaaaa, ababb, baabb, ababa, aabaa, baaba

8. aabbb, aabaa, babab

9. abbba, abbab, baaba, abaaa, abbab, abbaa

10. aaaab, ababa, aaaaa, aaaba, abaab
    ababb, aaaaa, aabba, abaaa, aaaba

II.

NATION-STATES

4

ENGLAND

{{{

Two powerful women faced each other in an intense rivalry with the throne of a growing empire as the prize. The series of plots and intrigues in the struggle between Mary, Queen of Scots and Elizabeth I of England involved ciphers that directly affected the final acts of this drama.

Born in 1533 and brought up as a Protestant, Elizabeth was the daughter of the notorious King Henry VIII and Anne Boleyn. Elizabeth ascended to the throne in 1558 amid numerous rumors and threats of schemes to depose her and put a Catholic on the throne. Fully aware of her tenuous position, Elizabeth gathered a very capable group of devoted followers. Among them was a contingent of people dedicated almost exclusively to securing intelligence. Numerous for their day, these fifty or so agents were carefully assigned according to their personal skills. Their leader was the master spy Sir Francis Walsingham.

Born in 1530 at Chislehurst, Kent, Walsingham studied at King's College, Cambridge. He made detailed studies of foreign languages, customs, and diplomatic traditions. His demonstrated abilities in Europe's courts gained him a knighthood in 1577 and the high position of Secretary of State soon thereafter. From this vantage point he was able to compile a list of all those who could endanger his queen. First among the names of threatening persons was that of Mary Stuart.

Mary was the daughter of Scotland's King James V and Mary of Guise. Born in 1542 at the Linlithgow Palace, she was Elizabeth's cousin. Even more important, she was next in succession to England's throne because Elizabeth had no children. But in spite of Mary's proximity to glory and power, few people in history led a more star-crossed existence. After the death of one husband, the murder of a second, and the flight of a third, Mary was forced by Scottish lords to leave her native land. Seeking Elizabeth's sympathy and protection, she instead was placed in virtual imprisonment for nineteen years by her cousin.

For reasons both personal and political, Elizabeth permitted her rival to remain alive. However, a number of people, including Walsingham, believed that Mary Stuart was gaining too much support among Catholics who believed Elizabeth to be a usurper. Trusted followers of Walsingham indicated that plans were being made to seize the crown for Mary. Yet such rumors were not enough to make Elizabeth sign a warrant for her kinswoman's death. She had to have proof. Therefore, Walsingham decided that he had to move directly to save Elizabeth and Protestantism as England's religion. He became *agent provocateur* in a conspiracy that linked the principal rivals and their supporters in what came to be known as the Babington Plot.

In 1586 Mary was being held at Chartley Castle in Stafford county. It was at this picturesque site that Walsingham chose to try to connect her directly in an attempt to depose Elizabeth. He sought to take advantage of both Mary's desire for liberty and the recklessly ambitious men who thought they could free her.

Among Walsingham's close associates in this effort was Thomas Phelippes. The son of London's customs collector, Phelippes's work for Walsingham and subsequent achievements earned him the title of England's first noteworthy cryptanalyst. Phelippes, who was about thirty years old at the time, had a knowledge of a number of verse forms and literary allusions. In addition, he could translate ciphers in French, Latin, Italian, and Spanish. Previously, at the request of Walsingham, he had traveled throughout the continent. This journey enabled him to educate himself in court customs and update Walsingham regarding the most recent spy and diplomatic tactics. Now, as the preparations for the trap began, Phelippes was ready to apply his uncanny skills with foreign tongues and messages.

Another member of the group was Gilbert Gifford. The son of a prominent Catholic family, Gifford had once trained for the priesthood. However, he had gone astray and abandoned this goal. He was facing a prison sentence when Walsingham intervened on his behalf. Quite willing to comply with his benefactor's wishes, Gifford agreed to use his religious background to gain the trust of the priests and Mary's followers. Pretending to be an ardent Catholic, Gifford gained the acquaintance of true believers on the continent and in England. Walsingham especially approved of Gifford's meetings with Anthony Babington.

In his mid-twenties, Babington was a boastful, wealthy adventurer. Born of a family with lineage to the Normans, he was secretly also a devout Catholic, and he had once been a page to Mary, Queen of Scots. Financially able to support a number of schemes, he vainly had begun to envision himself as Mary's champion. He had already formulated the groundwork of a plan to overthrow the government. With Walsingham's close guidance, Gifford fueled Babington's dream of gathering those devoted to securing freedom and the crown of England for Mary.

While young Babington began to gather his friends, Gifford posed as a cleric and patiently ingratiated himself with the lonely Chartley resident. He offered to help Mary exchange secret letters with her friends and even thought of a means to disguise this transfer of missives.

For a substantial fee, the local brewer, who supplied the Chartley castle staff, assumed an extra task. He agreed to conceal a leakproof box in a predetermined barrel or cask. Once the container was inside the castle, Gifford had one of his helpers bring the disguised correspondence to Mary. She in turn would place her letters in the container, which would then be taken beyond the walls in another barrel. This seemingly clever conveyance and Mary's desperate craving for help from others finally made her acquiesce to the barrel plan. Though wary, she did encipher her messages by using a *nomenclator,* the system that had a codelike list of words and names and a separate cipher alphabet. Mary's own name and her (supposedly) secret alphabet were written like this:

Mary   Stuart

Meanwhile, Anthony Babington, John Ballard, who was a zealous priest, and eleven other prime collaborators began to coalesce into a full-scale conspiracy plot.

The complicated effort included: the assassinations of Elizabeth, her minister William Cecil, and Walsingham; a ruse to free Mary from Chartley and take her to a safe haven; the seizure of the Royal Navy's ships guarding the Thames; and a call to arms for all true Catholics. During the general confusion and upheaval, help was to be sought from Catholic Philip II of Spain. Once the Protestant monarchy was completely toppled, Mary would be crowned Queen of England.

Caught up in the drama, Babington wanted Mary to know that he was the chief plotter. Naively depending on the barrel ploy and the disguised notes, he insisted that she recognize him by writing directly to him. In a damning message on July 12, he explained the details of Elizabeth's murder and Mary's deliverance. Again he asked for a personal reply from the Scots' Queen.

At this crucial point historians differ on pinpointing Mary's motivations for making an obviously endangering response. Some speculate that her reasoning powers were diminished by her many years of virtual isolation. After all, Babington and his cohorts were offering what appeared to be a dual dream come true: freedom and the crown. Other scholars of the time speculated that for all of her kindly ways, Mary must have had much animosity for her royal cousin. Having suffered so much, perhaps Mary's hatred logically could have risen to a level where it was not so difficult for her to contemplate the demise of her rival. Whatever the reasons, Mary decided to answer on July 17.

Thanks to Phelippes's and his own skills, Walsingham knew the exact contents of this crucial exchange as he had all the others. After Gifford had intercepted the barrel transfers long enough to copy them, Walsingham and Phelippes were able to decipher them in a matter of hours. What had appeared to be a trustworthy mask to the schemers was a thin veil indeed to the cryptanalysts, for two reasons.

First, the nomenclator was not a completely disguised cipher. It consisted of several factors, any one of which could serve as a weak point and thus reveal a pattern. Second, Walsingham and Phelippes had had a chance to see a number of messages with very similar word phrases, especially in the opening greetings and closing remarks. Both men knew about studies of letter frequency and looked for examples of repetition. Once they had found the telltale sequences, Walsingham and Phelippes must have reveled in their victory. When Mary replied, she fully incriminated herself in the following words:

```
    When your preparations both in England and
abroad are complete, let the six gentlemen who
have undertaken to assassinate Elizabeth pro-
ceed to their work, and when she is dead, then
come and set me free.
```

With the proof that Elizabeth needed for an official warrant of treason, Walsingham moved quickly to snuff the first flames of the uprising. Aware of the conspirators' movements, he had his men close in at several locations.

Each of the ill-fated band was found guilty and sentenced to be hanged, drawn, and quartered. Ballard and Babington were executed in this manner. However, upon hearing of the cruelty of their suffering, Elizabeth ordered that the others face only the hangman's noose. Nevertheless, she could extend no special mercy to her rival. Mary's direct complicity had become public knowledge. Beyond Elizabeth's own mixed emotions, political pressures, and the laws governing traitorous acts forced her to do what was expected of a threatened ruler.

Condemned by her own hand and a foolish dependency upon the nomenclator, Mary bravely faced her fate at Fotheringhay Castle in Northamptonshire, England. On February 8, 1587, at eight o'clock in the morning, the Queen of Scots knelt beneath the hands of a man named Bulle. He was a skilled executioner whose axe was swift and sure.

As fate would have it, another Stuart was to be undone, and ciphers were to play a key role once more. This Stuart was Mary's grandson, King Charles I. Like his grandmother, King Charles ruled at a very turbulent time in English history. He was born on November 19, 1600 and wore the crown when England's civil war began.

This conflict was the result of religious bickering, class differences, and political rivalries. The primary incidents revolved around Charles's disputes with Parliament and the rise of powerful royal competitors. These rivals were called the *Puritans* because of their desire to "purify" the Church of England. They were also derisively labeled the *Roundheads* because they chose to cut their hair shorter than the long-haired supporters of Charles, the *Cavaliers.*

When armed conflict began on August 22, 1642, the Puritans appeared to be outnumbered and not in a strategic position. The Cavaliers controlled most of England's large cities except London and much of the countryside, save for some sections along the eastern shore. However, the Puritans had two important "secret weapons."

Their first "weapon" was soon revealed: the brilliant leader and tactician, Oliver Cromwell. Using strict discipline, detailed training, and a keen mind for strategy, Cromwell molded the divided Puritans into an efficient fighting force. Soon the mocking nickname, Roundheads, began to strike fear into the Royalists. The Puritans' second "weapon" was a man who never pulled a bowstring or raised a sword in anger. His name was Sir John Wallis, and his only weapons were quill, ink, and paper. Yet the Cavaliers were soon to wish that he had carried a pike.

Wallis had been earning a living as a chaplain to a wealthy widow. His previously known gift for solving mathematical problems was presented with an unusual test. Knowing of his Puritan leanings, one of Oliver Cromwell's men brought Wallis a captured Cavalier message. When Wallis revealed its contents in short order, his interest in ciphers began.

Cromwell recognized his talents and quickly befriended him. Soon the general and the clergyman had combined their talents to help reverse the entire trend of the war. With Cavalier papers seized at the battle of Newbury, Wallis initiated a consecutive pattern of revelations that helped Cromwell in the field.

Throughout the struggle the Puritans had wanted to connect Charles to direct plots against members of Parliament. However, his Cavalier supporters had always managed to wage war without having their king appear to be directly involved. But this situation changed drastically after the discovery of some private correspondence.

On June 14, 1645, the parish of Naseby in Leicestershire was the site of a Puritan victory. Amid their rejoicing, Cromwell's men found a most interesting collection of letters among military dispatches captured from the Royalists. By this time it was customary to give such discoveries to Wallis. Hoping for some clues to the Cavaliers' next moves, the Roundheads were most pleasantly surprised by the news Wallis had for them. In this case the missives were much more valuable than the rival army's plans. Wallis had deciphered letters written by King Charles to his wife. In them he made statements that clearly defined his involvement in anti-Parliament schemes. As with his ancestor, Charles's false trust in ciphers initiated his demise. Four years later, largely on the basis of this type of evidence, the grandson of Mary Stuart was also beheaded.

Sir John Wallis was rewarded for his efforts by being granted the position of secretary to the Westminister Assembly. While in this respected post, he continued his deciphering work. Even after the civil war ended in 1652, the victorious Roundheads continued to bring him missives of all types. In their zealous desire for revenge, the Puritans constantly sought Cavaliers and their supporters. Yet even Wallis's considerable talents were not enough to help capture every one of the King's supporters. Ironically, it was another Sir John who figuratively kept his wits and thus literally kept his head.

Sir John Trevanion was a Royalist who had been captured and imprisoned by the Puritans. He was held in a castle in Colchester, a city on the southeastern coast of England. Because his fellow Cavaliers, Charles Lucas and George Lisle, had been executed before him, Trevanion was no doubt contemplating the hereafter as well.

While awaiting his fate, he received the following message from a friend:

```
Worthie Sir John:
    Hope, that is ye beste comfort of ye af-
flicted, cannot much, I fear me, help you now.
That I would say to you, is this only: if ever I
may be able to requite that I do owe you, stand
not upon asking me. 'Tis not much that I can do:
but what I can do, bee ye verie sure I wille. I
knowe that, if dethe comes, if ordinary men fear
it, it frights not you, accounting it for a high
honour, to have such a rewarde of your loyalty.
Pray yet that you may be spared this soe bitter,
cup. I fear not that you will grudge any suf-
ferings; only if bie submission you can turn them
away, 'tis the part of a wise man. Tell me, an
if you can, to do for you anythinge that you wolde
have done. The general goes back on Wednesday.
Restinge your servant to command.
                                        -R. T.
```

The identity of Trevanion's friend R. T. remains a historic mystery. There was apparently nothing suspicious about the missive for Trevanion's jailer. Even the reference to the unnamed general did not draw any unexpected scrutiny or keep the letter from being delivered to the prisoner's cell. But Trevanion found a simple yet cleverly hidden cipher within these words. The pattern of the cipher he found was this: the third letter located after each mark of punctuation spelled a message. Thus, the simple but profound message read: *panel at east end of chapel slides.*

Trevanion seemed to become very interested in prayer after finding this message. But what seemed to the Roundheads to be an hour of piety was actually sixty minutes that the clever Cavalier used to make good his escape.

5

FRANCE

⟨⟨⟨

The French kings, military planners, and nobility were aware of the value of secret writing and black chambers. With her broad, open borders, France had to be aware of shifts in allegiances, possible enemies, rising foreign leaders, threats to trade routes, and the like. More than its rival England, France was by its geographic situation bound to be embroiled in Europe's power struggles and intrigues.

As we have seen, France had a cipher scholar in Blaise de Vigenère. She also had a mathematician who came to the fore and helped his nation. He was François Viète, a counselor to the court of King Henry of Navarre.

Henry IV, a Protestant, was being confronted by the Holy League, a Catholic alliance. In 1589 this group's armies held many of the country's larger cities, aided by Catholic Philip of Spain. Just as Cromwell had his secret helper, so King Henry had one in Viète.

Viète was given some captured Spanish documents, and he broke the combination of letter substitutes, code words, and numbers. Though Henry did not get to make use of the information about enemy troop strength immediately, the revelations proved Viète's worth. After Henry had defeated his enemies, the mathematics expert was given his due credit and rewards for his success.

The next Frenchman with such clearly superior abilities also became known through a series of battles between Catholics and Huguenots, a group of French Protestants.

In 1628 Henry II, leader of a Catholic army, had surrounded Réalmont, a Huguenot bastion in southern France. The Protestant defenders appeared to be well entrenched. Henry, also known as the Prince of Condé, decided to bring up some cannons to try to breach the walls. Then, as so often happens in such situations, fortune changed.

Soldiers captured a citizen of Réalmont moving between the lines who was in possession of a cipher. The Prince of Condé and his advisers could not discern its meaning. But Henry had heard about a young fellow in a nearby town who possessed such skills. The man he sent for was Antoine Rossignol.

Rossignol did indeed have cryptanalytic skills, which he quickly applied to the cipher. He uncovered the fact that the Huguenots were in dire straits. Their apparent strength was misleading as they were asking for ammunition and weapons. When Henry confronted the Protestant leaders with what he knew, they soon chose to surrender.

Rossignol's success earned him a position with France's powerful Cardinal Richelieu. The cardinal had sent another Catholic army to besiege the Huguenot fortress of La Rochelle. Good luck remained with Richelieu's forces. They intercepted some enemy letters, and Rossignol "saw between their lines" to reveal that many in La Rochelle were hungry. Furthermore, English ships were expected to bring relief and extra firepower.

Thanks to Rossignol, the cardinal alerted his commanders. When the British ships arrived, they were faced with many cannons primed to fire. Unable to anchor in the harbor, the vessels stopped short. Threatened with starvation, the inhabitants of La Rochelle had to lay down their arms.

Thus, Rossignol became the original cryptologist of the Bourbon dynasty. Honors, increased wealth, and a country home were given to him. He was a favorite of Louis XIII and was often treated better than many of the nobles at court. His position was maintained when Louis XIV became king. He worked for this influential monarch during a golden era of French art, science, and philosophy.

Rossignol made an important contribution in his own field by directly altering the predominant nomenclator method. He knew it had a glaring weakness in that the coded and plaintext equivalents were alphabetized. Also, numbered codes were in numerical order. He disrupted this regimentation by shuffling the set patterns. This enabled him to mask documents for Louis XIV with at least two lists of plain and coded materials, which were alternately alphabetized or mixed. The concealment he made for Louis XIV came to be named the *Great Cipher*. It was considered unbreakable and indeed confounded other nations' experts for years thereafter.

To a lesser though nonetheless interesting extent, Louis also contributed to the secrecy of his field. Amidst the ostentatious trappings of his realm, the Sun King made his communications increasingly ornate. It could be said that he initiated a type of identity code for visitors and diplomats alike.

Passportlike forms were issued to visitors, with varied hues for each discernible nationality. The Dutch were issued a white paper, while Englishmen received yellow, and Russians pale green. These documents contained much more information about the person than was first obvious. Seemingly innocuous border patterns and designs revealed facts about the individual.

For example, suppose that a baron from one of the German principalities arrived in Paris. At the department where the visitors' papers were issued, a clerk would make a list of pertinent facts about the baron. His social position, wealth, age, opinions, marital status, religion, and many other such details would be recorded. Then other workers at the office would create the person's "identity" paper. Cutting it in rectangular or oval shapes indicated age brackets such as 25–35 or 45–55. A different type of flower in one of the corners, or the top or bottom of the oval, identified the baron's feelings as friendly, antagonistic, or something in between. A thin, colored ribbon tied through narrow holes revealed whether he was single or married. His wealth was indicated by designs around the edges. Patterns of strokes beneath the baron's name showed his height and weight. Punctuation marks identified his religious preference (e.g., a comma meant Protestant). Factors such as particular talents, intelligence, and honesty could be depicted too. Such a form might have looked like this:

After the baron was issued his official paper, he was expected to present it as a kind of calling card to strangers. Let us suppose that he wished to have an audience with Cardinal Mazarin, Richelieu's successor.

A servant would bring the paper to the cardinal's quarters. Having seen such forms innumerable times, Mazarin would look for the details that most interested him in order to facilitate his busy day of decision-making. Perhaps the baron's wealth or connections in Europe could be beneficial in some way to the monarchy, in which case the baron would be "granted an audience." On the other hand, indicators of a religious difference or even a brusque personality might get the paper and its bearer a quick refusal. Of course, such a procedure might lead to prejudiced responses. But those in power, like Mazarin, often preferred this identity code to the more costly, time-consuming background checks made by spies. The French paper-making clerks were trusted to be honest since their livelihood and their very lives could be jeopardized by mistakes.

Forgeries were sometimes attempted. The temptation to create a paper that would gain access to powerful court favor was strong indeed. However, there were many safeguards in the form of special papers, ribbons, designs, and wax seals used. Additionally, a visitor had to be wary of everything from social ostracism to expulsion, and painful months in a dungeon or worse for being caught in a lie. Thus, until better methods of verifying one's background came to be accepted and proved more practical, King Louis's identity code was to serve his nation's security needs well.

Even though the Great Cipher protected communications, Rossignol monitored others' missives, and the Sun King's code labeled visitors, France's borders were not free of intrigue. In 1674 greed and stifled ambition led to a case of treason and the failure to discern a lifesaving cipher.

The 1670s saw a number of problems arising between the French and the increasingly influential Dutch to the north. The Bourbon dynasty was so concerned that it increased its troop strength and heavily armed the forts all along its defense perimeter.

One of the strategic sites was the bastion of Quilleboeuf, which was commanded by Chevalier de Rohan. The Chevalier had a high social position, and he also had a reputation for being a code solver who exchanged short coded notes with admirers. Although the fortress and the town were strategically located, de Rohan was not satisfied. His desire for money and a higher rank led him into a conspiracy. The Chevalier plotted with his friend and assistant, Trouaumont, to betray Quilleboeuf to the Dutch.

With Trouaumont acting as a go-between, arrangements were made for payments by the Dutch in exchange for treasonous information. While de Rohan waited for his friend to return with the payment,

Trouaumont was shot, and then both plotters were arrested and locked in separate cells.

The Chevalier refused to admit that he was a traitor. His captors seemed to have no positive proof against him. Yet he could not be certain about Trouaumont. His coconspirator had lived, but had he recovered sufficiently to talk? When he did, would he be persuaded by threat or torture to reveal their plans? Would his friend become his most dangerous enemy by divulging all he knew to spare himself?

The Chevalier might have learned much more if he had included a code called the *quadrilateral alphabet* among his assorted interests. This alphabet had been known in similar forms by prisoners in various countries for years. Its English version had five groups of five letters (*z* was omitted). Its popularity with prisoners was due to the fact that it could be conveyed audibly.

An incarcerated person first rapped on a wall or the cell's bars to attract the attention of the nearby recipient. Once the prearranged return signal was heard, the quadrilateral alphabet could commence.

Beginning taps indicated the letter group: for example, a solitary sound signified the group *a* to *e;* 2 taps were for *f* to *j,* and so forth. But how did one know the specific letters? The following partial list, with the dashes (—) representing pauses, gives an idea of how the quadrilateral alphabet sounded:

$$
\begin{aligned}
\textit{Tap—Tap} &= \text{A} \\
\textit{Tap—Tap, Tap} &= \text{B} \\
\textit{Tap, Tap—Tap} &= \text{F} \\
\textit{Tap, Tap—Tap, Tap} &= \text{G} \\
\textit{Tap, Tap, Tap—Tap} &= \text{K} \\
\textit{Tap, Tap, Tap—Tap, Tap} &= \text{L}
\end{aligned}
$$

One had to listen carefully to discern the noise sequences in the dank, echo-filled dungeons. Without looking at the previous examples, answer quickly. Which letter is given by four taps, then two? What is five taps, then three? The answers are: *q* (group four, second letter) and *w* (group five, third letter).

The Bourbon authorities believed that de Rohan and Trouaumont were guilty. They did their best to make the suspected traitors turn on each other by breaking their will power. After all, their captors reasoned, if they were willing to betray their nation for a few thousand livres, would one or the other not be willing to talk to avoid torture and execution?

Shortly before the Chevalier confronted the eventful day, he received a bundle of clothing, in which he found a note attached to a shirt sleeve. The note contained a ciphered phrase made up of these letters:

```
MG EULHXCCLGU GHJ YXUJ LM CT ULGC ALJ.
```

Possibly de Rohan wondered if this were some kind of ruse to trick him. He continued to remain puzzled as he struggled against time to unravel the letters. The man who had claimed cipher skills had failed to find the real meaning.

Feverish with frustration, perhaps unbalanced by guilt and regret, the Chevalier was unnerved when he was brought into the presence of his accusers. Quickly broken by the prosecutor's harsh questions, he gave a full confession and the judges ordered him to meet his executioner.

And what of Trouaumont's fate? His fellow conspirator's testimony would not have harmed de Rohan. Had de Rohan been able to discern what was a basic substitution cipher, he would have known why and also saved himself in the process. He could have done so, because the note he received said in French:

```
Le prisonnier est mort; il n'a rien dit.
```
(The prisoner is dead; he said nothing.)

Trouaumont, though a traitor to his country, had remained loyal to his friend and had died with their secret intact. This final, bitter irony was revealed to de Rohan just before his execution.

The Sun King's agents had succeeded in exposing this conspiracy. Yet within just a few more years, Louis's own communications were to be threatened by skilled eyes. With Rossignol's passing, the Great Cipher was not always applied to royal correspondence. This carelessness was to bode ill for the French royalty. The threat to its most guarded secrets came from England's master cryptanalyst, Sir John Wallis.

King Charles II had returned to the British throne in 1660, and Wallis had remained the chief code breaker. Oliver Cromwell's successes had made a lasting impression on the Cavaliers. Charles II wanted such proven expertise close at hand, and he appointed Wallis to be his chaplain.

Wallis continued his lengthy public service into the reign of William and Mary. During that time he reported to the Earl of Nottingham. As King William's Secretary of War, Nottingham was in charge of protecting the nation from all threats, external and internal. Thus, he worked closely with Wallis.

It was this effort that reaped substantial benefits in the 1680s. Wallis was able to lift the shroud covering the correspondence between Louis XIV and the French ambassador in Poland. Since it was not protected by the Great Cipher, this accomplishment arguably could be considered average for Wallis. However, the results were of high-level importance.

One of the letters revealed that Louis was scheming with Poland's king to form an alliance and declare war on Prussia. Because this union threatened the balance of power in Europe, it was also dangerous to England. Wallis knew that William wanted the European nations divided and France as completely isolated as possible. Therefore, when he uncovered the French communiqués, he realized that he was holding powerful information. Nottingham agreed and went directly to King William.

A shrewd practitioner of court intrigue, William found ways to make the secret diplomacy public. The results were quite damaging to Louis XIV. Not only did his scheme to attack Prussia fail, but the French ambassador corps was expelled from Poland and the Polish were alienated for several years thereafter. Prussia, rarely unprepared for war, became even more militant. To William's great pleasure, the continental powers were at odds, and Louis XIV was left to sulk in the disgrace of his exposed plans.

So far history has not provided any evidence to indicate that Antoine Rossignol and Sir John Wallis ever competed directly within the rivalry between their countries. The Great Cipher was not specifically created to fool Wallis, nor was Wallis ordered to devote all his formidable talents to breaking it. Perhaps he might have succeeded had he been given the opportunity. The time when such individuals matched minds directly or in groups was several decades away.

6

PRUSSIANS, POTENTATES, AND PHILOSOPHERS

↠

The seventeenth and early eighteenth centuries saw a variety of approaches to codes, ciphers, and secret languages. They ranged from rulers' personal systems to efficient black chambers, and the special languages of fraternal organizations.

One potentate with a private method of communication was Sultan Ibrahim. This powerful man ruled the vast Turkish empire in the mid-1600s. Curiously, he chose to set up the only known code of his reign because of his especially large harem. Even more unusual, it may be the only known olfactory code on record.

The Sultan enjoyed recalling rendezvous with his concubines in all corners of his palace and grounds. To heighten the enjoyment of his recollections and the anticipation of his next tryst, he ordered his best alchemists to develop a series of different perfumes, to represent each of his different romantic encounters.

But women also had their effect on codes and ciphers, and one such influential woman was Maria Theresa, empress of the Holy Roman Empire. Much like England's Queen Elizabeth in her awareness of international events, Maria was a ruler of action. She helped her nation by taking a direct interest in Austria's black chamber, the *Geheime Kabinets-Kanzlei* in Vienna.

Because Vienna was a great cultural center and a geographic crossroads of Europe, Austria's rulers and generals alike carefully studied goods, travelers, and mail passing through the city. They tried to know about everything and everyone of importance that moved between western Europe's capitals to places like Constantinople and St. Petersburg. Maria Theresa not only made certain that the *Kabinets-Kanzlei* was well funded, she also gave pertinent advice to Austrian diplomats who used the secrets of the chamber. She warned them not to use the same codes too often. Such was her knowledge of the field that she suggested they apply new keys more often to fool potential enemies.

With the backing of the empress, effective bonus rewards for solutions, and incentives of promotions, the Austrians' black chamber became a model of efficiency and volume. Their system operated like a private business before the times of capitalist principles.

Early in the morning the mail meant for foreign embassies was instead taken to the chamber. There, groups of people initiated a series of tasks that included: opening letters (often melting seals); transcribing potentially important sections; dictating lengthy missives; translating (if needed); replacing letters in their original folds with forged seals; and returning letters to the mail.

At the height of its productivity, from the 1730s to the 1760s, the *Kabinets-Kanzlei* was considered by many to be the finest such organization in Europe. It is interesting that historians praise its finest director, Baron de Koch, not for the particular skills of a Wallis or a Rossignol but for his administrative abilities and respect for his personnel. Still, he achieved his goals largely through the power he wielded as secretary to Maria Theresa. Thanks to her and to the Baron's planning, their Vienna operation was centuries ahead of its time.

However, in spite of this obvious success, the very smooth compiling of facts led to a major setback. Even more surprising, this reversal was not discovered by the Austrians for years.

In 1774 King Louis XV, whose great grandfather had been jolted by the Wallis revelations, got a chance to have a cipher coup of his own. Because a loyal Frenchman in Vienna had been alert and had some ready coins, Louis XV was given an unexpected advantage.

The Bourbon supporter was Abbot Georgel, the secretary of France's ambassador in Austria. He was able to buy a highly prized bundle of papers and send them by an experienced courier to Louis XV.

When the King opened the package, even he was surprised by the contents. They were the neatly ordered and efficiently compiled results of very recent *Kabinets-Kanzlei* deciphering successes. His majesty even found copies of some of his own missives. The very compact, ordered, and correct records of the *Kabinets-Kanzlei* had made them quite tempting and open to theft by a clever turncoat. The man who contacted Abbot Georgel was apparently never identified. The Abbot was rewarded for his efforts and Louis XV decided to apply the Great Cipher more frequently to protect himself from England to the west and the efficient Austrians to the east.

The Austrians and the French both had to be aware of the duchies and principalities to the north such as Hesse, Saxony, and Schleswig-Holstein. One of the more curious stories of this period about codes and ciphers was linked to the Prussian province of Brandenburg. It involved an official who greatly benefited not from a cipher's revelation but from a mistake.

Frederick, Elector of Brandenburg, ruled this duchy in eastern Prussia during the early 1700s. An ambitious man, he desired to increase his holdings and eventually hoped to rule a kingdom. However, to accomplish this sizable task, he needed the approval of the Holy Roman Emperor as well as the powerful Catholic church.

Frederick had a representative in Vienna. He also had friends among the Jesuits there. He often corresponded with these men in a cipher that included numbers for individuals. Frederick gave himself #24. One of his best Jesuit friends, Father Wolf, was designated #116. The emperor, Leopold I, was #110.

The Viennese representative finally sent a message to the Elector saying that an opportune moment was at hand. He was told to begin correspondence with #_ _ _ right away. This news would have been perfect but for the numbers being distorted. Was it #110 or #116? Frederick couldn't discern the smeared numerals. Nor did he want to miss the chance to act. Assuming that the number must be 116, or Father Wolf, he then composed a lengthy letter to the Jesuit.

It contained humble but well-phrased plans for changing the duchy's status. Frederick took the gamble of expressing his allegiance to Catholicism. In those years, when Protestants were increasing their support all across Europe, his position was risky. Still, he put his beliefs on paper and asked for religious guidance. He sent it without consulting with his representative.

Father Wolf was quite impressed with the missive. So pleased was he that he showed it to the leader of Vienna's Jesuits. The chief of the order was also very pleased. By means of his own links to other church officials, Frederick's wishes were presented in formal proceedings to the emperor himself. This representation by Catholic dignitaries was meaningful even to the sometimes haughty Leopold. In fact, because he too depended on the church for a large part of his support, he could not easily refuse.

To avoid offending his Catholic friends, Leopold agreed to make the Brandenburg region a kingdom. A realm had to have a ruler. Frederick's dream became a reality when he was crowned king. Neither he nor the Vienna agent who had smeared the numbers could have imagined such success: a cipher mistake had made a monarch.

While embroiled in trying to unmask each others' intentions, most of the nation-states of continental Europe sooner or later looked to the East. Certainly they sought better routes to China, Japan, and India for silks, spices, tea, and jewels. But in terms of military and political alliances, heads of state often gazed warily at the vast land mass that was Russia.

Prussia and the countries from Poland to Turkey had a direct interest in the secretive events occurring in St. Petersburg. Russia's long borders shared with the countries of Eastern Europe were the sites of frequent dispute. Everything from territorial claims to personal grudges tended to provide the sparks of warfare.

From the view of Russia's Czars, Europe's kingdoms were at their best when they were divided and fighting among themselves. Any alliances, especially strong ones, were a threat to more than one Czar's designs. Expansion into warmer climates and the search for year-round, ice-free ports had become a virtual obsession among Russia's leaders since the Renaissance. By the 1700s the Czars were trying to form their own pacts with Europe's crowned heads in order to protect the same borders that others watched.

Peter the Great, who ruled from 1682 to 1725, is considered an enlightened Czar because he tried to open Russia to Western science, art, crafts, and so on. It also is highly probable that it was his wisdom that brought more credible cryptology to his homeland. Before his reign, the methods used were crude at best. They were decades, if not centuries, behind those of Wallis, Rossignol, and the *Kabinets-Kanzlei.*

History does not record exactly where Pëtr Alekseyevich may have learned about the actual methods of the efficient black chambers. He was interested in the mechanics of everything from map making to ship building, and Europe's expanding guilds. Certainly, knowing how well other countries managed codes and ciphers would have been enough to make his eager mind ever more curious. It is also possible that the scholars and craftsmen he brought back from Europe to teach his people may have included a cryptologist or two.

Still, Russia's backwardness in cryptology did not change overnight. Simple substitutions with supposedly indiscernible symbols continued to be used into the 1720s. Through the reigns of his daughter, Elizaveta Petrovna, and then the German-born empress Catherine II (Catherine the Great), Russia's cipher makers matured. With nomenclators of more than a thousand parts, their creations finally rivaled many of Europe's best in the mid-1700s.

As the Russian populace became more dissatisfied with the government of the Czars, secret organizations grew, their ranks made up of those who wanted to change political life in Russia, their families, and the relatives of those killed in the struggle.

Oddly enough, one of the more popular means of communication for this underground army was very similar to the quadrilateral alphabet of de Rohan's era. Perhaps similar people, enraged at Europe's own autocrats, shared their methods with each other. Whatever the actual linkage, Russian rebels and prisoners alike shared an audible code.

This code was almost exactly like the quadrilateral in its use of rapping on walls, pipes, or the like to signal letter positions. Because the Russian language employs the Cyrillic alphabet, which has more than thirty letters, this process was somewhat more complicated. Here are examples of the most frequently used Cyrillic letters and their English equivalents:

CYRILLIC—ENGLISH ALPHABET

Cyrillic	English	Cyrillic	English	Cyrillic	English
А а	a	Й й	i or y	У у	u
Б б	b	К к	k	Ф ф	f
В в	v	Л л	l	Х х	kh
Г г	g or gh	М м	m	Ц ц	ts
Д д	d	Н н	n	Ч ч	ch
Е е	e or ye	О о	o	Ш ш	sh
Ё ё	e or yo	П п	p	Ы ы	y
Ж ж	zh	Р р	r	Э э	e
З з	z	С с	s	Ю ю	yu
И и	i or y	Т т	t	Я я	ya or ia

Assume that the thirty letters are separated into five groups of six letters each, the five divisions being as follows:

1. **А**   **Е**
2. **Ё**   **К**
3. **Л**   **Р**
4. **С**   **Ц**
5. **Ч**   **Я**

We can proceed to send messages with the quadrilateral pattern and the alphabet differences in mind. Remember that dashes (—) mean a pause in the sounds:

Tap—Tap = **А**
Tap—Tap, Tap = **Б**
Tap, Tap, Tap—Tap = **Л**
Tap, Tap, Tap—Tap, Tap, Tap, Tap, Tap, Tap = **Р**
Tap, Tap, Tap, Tap, Tap—Tap = **Ч**
Tap, Tap, Tap, Tap, Tap—Tap, Tap = **Ш**

Prisoners also developed an aural cipher of taps that equated numbers with letters. Its six columns and five rows formed a Cyrillic checkerboard similar to the Polybius square. Memorized number/letter combinations eventually made "conversations" quite rapid.

With the growth of the Russians' skills, the nations of Eurasia found themselves on a rather balanced cryptological scale between successful concealment and the risk of disclosure by the 1750s.

7

SECRETS AND SIGNS

⟨⟨⟨

While nation-states vied for influence and alliances, secret societies used ciphers and codes to bridge boundaries between peoples. Such codes instilled an intense kind of loyalty among their members. In addition to these societies, we shall consider one man, an abbot, who created a special language all its own. But first, let us begin with the organizations.

The origins of some of these groups go back to the uncertain records of the Middle Ages. They have been included in the time frame of the 1700s because their ranks had grown large enough by then to make them influential. Some national leaders and policy makers were members themselves or had friends who were.

One of these societies, which maintained a high level of secrecy for many decades, was the Rosicrucians. A scholarly and religiously oriented group, their full name was the Ancient Mystical Order Rosae Crucis (AMORC). Their beginnings in the fifteenth century are somewhat shrouded in myth and legend. Some historic sources refer to the fifteenth-century man named Christian Rosenkreuz or Rosenkreutz (German for "rosy cross"). The group purportedly chose their symbol and special seal, a cross bearing a rose, from the name of this sage.

However, the Rosicrucians themselves are far from unified in their acceptance of this individual or such an explanation. A few of their historians say he was only a personage of folklore. Others in the order believe that he may have existed when the German-speaking duchies began to show a growing interest in the movement. According to them, he might have founded a lodge, perhaps even the first lodge, in a principality that one day would become a unified Germany.

Another debate within the group centers around a book of secret writings called the *Fama*. Some thought its contents regarding mankind were heretical. Others believed it presented an enlightened message of truth. The actual thoughts are not as important to understanding the order's background as is the reputed author of this book. Some say he was the mysterious Rosenkreuz. Others believe that though Rosenkreuz may have written a pamphlet called the *Fama Fraternitatis,* it was one Johann Valentin Andreä who wrote the more detailed *Fama.*

Rosicrucians who favor this account claim that Andreä was born on August 17, 1586, at Würtemberg. They believe that he received Lutheran theological and philosophic training with noted teachers at respected sites of that day. Furthermore, they credit him with certain mystical sayings and prophecies. Their purpose in clearly defining Andreä's life seems to be the placing of the Christian Rosenkreuz in the realm of legend. After all, how could he have written the *Fama* when he supposedly lived in the 1400s? Because of the script style of the *Fama,* it would have to have been written after 1500.

Historians and archivists not associated with AMORC give a different account. They recognize the existence of the *Fama Fraternitatis* as an anonymous pamphlet. It was printed in Kassel, a city in a west central German province, in 1614. It is this material that is said to contain the first reference to the Rosicrucians. The pamphlet told how Rosenkreuz was taught in a monastery and traveled the world of Islam to learn the secrets of the universe. He then started the Rose Cross monastic order and swore its members to secrecy by sacred oath. They promised to devote themselves to world renewal and peace through a joining of religious faith and scientific fact.

Two years later another account, the *Chymische Hochzeit,* appeared. This was reputedly the story of Rosenkreuz as an elderly prophetlike fellow and was written by Rosenkreuz himself. Some years after 1616 however, the Lutheran Johann Andreä confessed that he had created this material as a young man's lark. Some researchers now believe he may have written one or both of the previously mentioned *Fama* texts as well.

Whatever the reality of the events in the 1600s, many AMORC members may have preferred to deny the Rosenkreuz accounts for another reason. They would rather place their origins much earlier in history. Because several of their symbols, beliefs, and rituals have references to the ancient Egyptians, loyal followers find many connections to that advanced civilization. Everything from the mysteries of the Sphinx and the pyramids to the obviously far-sighted knowledge of the Nile dwellers is incorporated as part of their historic foundation. Though no one forefather or single family tree is mentioned, references to Pharaohs and wise men alike are given in Rosicrucian texts.

The original Egyptian organization was known as the Great White Lodge, but AMORC studies have placed it at more than one location among the ancient sites. At this place they believe that special knowledge, known as the *Osirian mysteries,* was discussed and perhaps actually revealed for the first time. These teachings relating to the god Osiris were believed to contain the answers to many of life's questions. Yet, only a chosen few *illuminati* were ever given this wisdom. Chief priests, referred to as *Kheri Hebs,* recorded these mystical facts on carefully guarded papyri. This secret knowledge was handed down to other chosen ones, called *adepts* or *initiates.* It was they who began decades of questing to found worship centers and schools in the lands bordering the Mediterranean. Eventually, having organizations of their own, they began the separate practice of the Rose Cross orders.

In spite of charges that occult and pagan rituals were being fostered, the AMORC grew in membership. Chapters spread as formal education made its way from Greece, north and east and across the Balkans to Italy. Rosicrucian records and other histories do validate a series of persecutions, raids upon chapter dwellings, ostracism, and so forth. Like many other such groups, they were frequently the target of prejudice and misunderstanding, though neither their theories nor their aims were necessarily threatening to any society.

The Rosicrucians believed that everything was linked to a divine being. The cross was their central symbol. Their goals included earthly peace and the wise use of science. They believed that once man is aware of the divine nature within himself, he can become a microcosm of the universe. With such wisdom, he can begin to affect the energies and forces around him. When controlling these powers, he can work positively against evil.

Rather than being unusual, revolutionary, or atheistic, doctrines of this type were both known and practiced in varied ways by Greek scholars, Hermetic sages, Gnostic philosophers in Egypt, and Hindu wise men. Such philosophies were kept alive by loyal devotees, much as Christianity was preserved during the Dark Ages. The Rosicrucians emerged from this time of upheaval stronger and more unified than ever.

With the passing of the Middle Ages, the Rosicrucians list philosophers such as Descartes and royalty such as Louis XIII as believers. By the 1700s the order had moved to the Americas where the influential Thomas Jefferson was among its supporters. With such people heeding at least some of their teachings, AMORC had become an influential society world wide. Through the lean and the bountiful years, its leaders continued private correspondences. These missives traveled great distances with a simple cipher that baffled outsiders. Indeed, some of Europe's best cryptanalysts were never able to break it. This is the method that fooled a number of experts:

⊏ ⊡ ⌐ ⌊ ⌋ ⊏ ⌐ ⌋ ⌊ ⌋ ⊡ ⌐

With four of the figures repeating, can you identify the frequency pattern and thus unmask the message? Bear in mind that these symbols may or may not indicate letters. Thus, repetition may not be such a good clue. This factor was one of the largest barriers for cipher solvers. Did these symbols equate with letters, numbers, or other figures that matched up with some alphabet? Perhaps they were more similar to hieroglyphs or *runes,* an ancient Scandinavian alphabet. More than one sage in the black chambers remained stumped as long as this angle was pursued.

Actually, the Rosicrucians' cipher had the advantage of being self-referential. It did not require either a key that was difficult to remember or a code word that was possible for an outsider to uncover. The real success of the system lay in its simplicity. In its original form, using the English alphabet, it was set up as follows:

A B C	D E F	G H I
J K L	M N O	P Q R
S T U	V W X	Y Z

On a simple grid, the positions of the letters follow the standard alphabet from a to z. Other patterns could be used if predetermined by both sender and recipient. In this standard example, each letter is represented by the shape of the "box" or partial "box" formed by the grid and by a dot positioned where the letter would be. The first three letters are:

A ⸬⌋   B ⸬⌉   C ⌋·

The a's dot is in the first position, or left side; b is second in the middle; and c is third on the right. The letters d, e, and f are differentiated by the shape of the grid's lines, as follows:

D |·⌋   E |·⌋   F |·⌋

Here we see that the easy-to-recall pattern of dots in order across the grid is varied by the shape of the "box." Actually, the only completely "boxed" letters are m, n, and o:

M [·]   N [·]   O [·]

Still, the variety is maintained by the grid's sides through the completed alphabet.

V ⌈·⌉   W ⌈·⌉   X ⌈·⌉   Y ⌈·   Z ·⌉

Now that you understand the method, can you decipher the original AMORC example? It is *Rosicrucians*.

R   O   S   I   C   R   U   C   I   A   N   S

Eventually, as some disenchanted individuals left the order and broke their vows of secrecy, this cipher was revealed. Nevertheless, it is curious that it fooled so many for so long. Rosicrucian societies continue to flourish today in America and Europe, although they no longer use such ciphers.

Another organization that expanded during this time was the Free and Accepted Masons.

The origins of the Freemasons, or Masons, as they are generally known, are more clearly defined than those of the Rosicrucians. The Masons were originally stoneworkers who came to prominence by building cathedrals and other such edifices between 850 and 1650 A.D. They joined with other builders in workers' groups called *guilds*. These associations came into existence for mutual protection and eventually set a kind of quality standard among their members.

This connection to medieval times and the attempts by some historians to link the Masons to the Egyptian pyramid builders caused temporary confusion in determining the starting point for the organization. However, unlike the Rosicrucians, the Masons have a specific date by which they can chart their formal association. That date is June 24, 1717.

On this day four builders' groups met in London. Because some of them referred to their memberships as *lodges,* the four combined and picked the title, the Masonic Grand Lodge.

This fraternal body chose builders' tools as symbols. They believed in the brotherhood of mankind within God's guidance and used the precepts of many religions. They considered God to be the architect of the universe. Though not a specific denomination, the Masons fostered charitable efforts and gave instructions for self-improvement. In all of these regards, they were quite open in their public dealings. They were more secretive when it came to the membership initiations and certain rituals.

Freemasonry gained a strong foothold in the British colonies among the craftsmen who were needed in the New World. By 1730 lodges had been set up in both Philadelphia and Boston. Benjamin Franklin was a prominent member of the Pennsylvania colony, and in 1734 he printed the first Masonic text for the Western Hemisphere. Among the generation of leaders who won freedom from England, George Washington, John Hancock, and Paul Revere were Masons.

The secrecy of the Masons that so upset many people was actually nothing more than the right of a private organization to conduct its own nonharmful business away from public scrutiny. Though many remained suspicious of the Masons, the society flourished. Eventually, time, perhaps carelessness on the part of some Masons, and certainly the loose tongues of former members combined to reveal their own special cipher.

Their method would not have been a secret to the Rosicrucians, however, not because the AMORC members were stellar cryptanalysts but because their ciphers had almost the same pattern. Though the Masons occasionally added some abbreviations and symbolic drawings, their method was essentially the same:

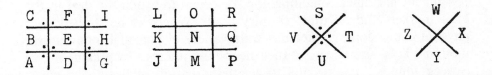

Now that you are familiar with the Rosicrucians' system, use this one to decipher the following phrase and learn a Masonic term:

⌐· ⌐ ∧ ⊓· □ ⌐ ⊔ ⊓ ⌐ □·

If you interpreted this properly, you now know the name of the Mason's basic organization. It is the first level on which a newly accepted member joins, the *Blue Lodge.*

Decoding this message probably seemed relatively simple with experience and with the full cipher chart before you. But imagine having neither and being confronted with the lines and dots above. No wonder the Masons seemed so strange and mysterious to the uninitiated.

Before concluding this chapter, we need to leave the 1820s and return to the early 1700s. We go back to Europe and stop at Versailles, France. There on November 25, 1712, a most unusual man was born. He was not one of the royalty; rather, he entered the world in humble surroundings. Yet unlike more than one blue blood whose contributions to the nation were questionable, this individual provided others with a unique tool. He devised a means of overcoming a heretofore insurmountable handicap: his creation was a sign language for the hearing-impaired.

Charles Michel de l'Épée was an abbot who frequently journeyed between Paris and the town of Troyes. On one such return trip to Paris he stopped at the home of a parishioner. There he met her two daughters, both of whom were deaf. He was deeply moved by the sight of these charming young women who were unable to hear a sound. Yet, though his heart was heavy, his mind was alert to the beginning of an idea. In the girls' awkward attempts to communicate by waving, facial expressions, nods, and touching, he had a vision that extended beyond their mother's parlor.

After further quiet contemplation, he began to watch the deaf in the Paris markets and on quiet country roads. Wherever he studied their physical expressions, he noted a wide variety of personal, nonuniform motions. They also vocalized their needs and interests by making noises (speech sounds, knocks, etc.) to get the attention of those who could hear. To l'Épée, their efforts seemed to be an attempt at communicating a series of linked ideas like sentences.

His vision to help the deaf communicate began to clarify and take shape in the form of one-handed gestures. Having watched all kinds of pointing, crossing of fingers, and clapping for attention, Abbé de l'Épée came to the conclusion that five fingers, if held and moved in various planned ways, could express a wider range of meanings. If these positions were equated with letters of the alphabet, whole words were within one's grasp. With words, the deaf had speech in the palms of their hands.

The two young women became his pupils. With their help he was able to apply his one-handed alphabet. The sisters were able to converse in a systematic way for the first time in their lives. The abbot could see his theory become a reality. By the time they had each mastered the alphabet, de l'Épée was correcting the rough spots. He also was taught by them as he learned the meanings of gestures they had used before. To the girls' mother and their village friends, the full development of this astonishing secret language was a godsend. By the most effective communication of all, word of mouth, the news of Abbé de l'Épée spread rapidly.

In 1755 de l'Épée began a school for the hearing- and speech-impaired. Using his own meager funds, he equipped the learning center with fundamental necessities. From among priests and public instructors, he began a new struggle to recruit volunteer teachers and won the favor of Louis XVI. The tiny school was funded from the royal coffers and grew to become a major institution in Paris.

In 1776 de l'Épée published a book regarding his sign language and the proper instruction of the deaf and the mute. He was writing a more elaborate dictionary of hand signs when he died in December 1789.

More involved sign languages have since been created, but when one recalls the almost nonexistent training of the hearing-impaired two-hundred years ago, his achievement is all the more remarkable. Here is a representation of l'Épée's one-handed alphabet and its English-alphabet equivalents:

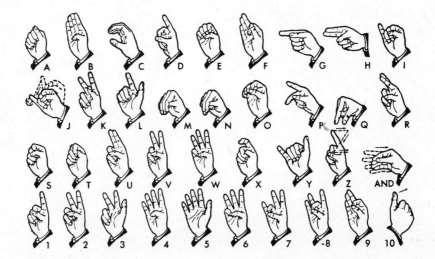

CRYPTANALYST'S CHAMBER II

QUIZ I

Mary, Queen of Scots was quite familiar with these people and places. Use her secret alphabet to learn about them. (Answers on page 256.)

1. $w\,a\,b\,R\,t\,k\,H\,o \quad w\,b\,b\,t\,k\,H$

2. $\amalg\,b\,k\,b\,\sigma\,\omega\,f\,a\,b\,\sigma$

3. $g\,b\,g\,\sigma\,\omega\,f\,t\,x\,\omega \quad \infty\,k\,x\,t$

4. $\infty\,a\,H\,k\,\sigma\,\infty\,\infty\,H\,b$

5. $g\,b\,k\,k\,b\,R\,m$

6. $b\,w\,x\,t\,k\,b\,\omega\,m$

7. $\infty\,a\,\sigma\,k\,\sigma\,\infty \quad x\,\upsilon\,b\,\infty\,b\,\sigma\,\omega$

8. $H\,k\,\sigma\,r\,t\,b\,g\,H\,t\,a$

9. $f\,\sigma\,\upsilon\,\upsilon\,x\,R\,m$

10. $\upsilon\,x\,t\,a\,H\,R\,\sigma\,\omega\,f\,a\,b\,o \quad w\,b\,b\,t\,k\,H$

QUIZ 2

With the lessons learned from de Rohan's debacle in chapter 5, can you translate these sounds from the next cell into your own escape plan? *Note:* Each section of taps represents one word spelled vertically. (Answers on page 256.)

Tap, Tap, Tap—Tap =
Tap—Tap, Tap, Tap, Tap, Tap =
Tap, Tap, Tap, Tap, Tap—Tap, Tap, Tap, Tap, Tap =

Tap, Tap—Tap, Tap, Tap, Tap =
Tap, Tap, Tap—Tap, Tap, Tap, Tap =

Tap, Tap, Tap, Tap, Tap—Tap, Tap, Tap =
Tap—Tap =
Tap, Tap, Tap—Tap, Tap =
Tap, Tap, Tap—Tap, Tap =

Tap—Tap, Tap, Tap =
Tap, Tap, Tap, Tap—Tap, Tap, Tap =
Tap—Tap, Tap, Tap, Tap, Tap =
Tap, Tap, Tap, Tap, Tap—Tap, Tap =
Tap, Tap—Tap, Tap, Tap, Tap =
Tap—Tap, Tap, Tap =
Tap—Tap, Tap, Tap, Tap, Tap =

QUIZ 3

Your benefactor in the next cell has heard you find the key. But you can't have "great expectations" until you can decipher his second aural message. (Answers on page 256.)

Tap—Tap,Tap, Tap =
Tap—Tap, Tap, Tap, Tap, Tap =
Tap, Tap, Tap—Tap, Tap =
Tap, Tap, Tap—Tap, Tap =
Tap—Tap =
Tap, Tap, Tap, Tap—Tap, Tap, Tap =

Tap, Tap, Tap, Tap, Tap—Tap, Tap, Tap =
Tap—Tap, Tap, Tap, Tap, Tap =
Tap, Tap, Tap—Tap, Tap =
Tap, Tap, Tap—Tap, Tap =

Tap, Tap, Tap, Tap—Tap, Tap, Tap, Tap =
Tap, Tap, Tap, Tap, Tap—Tap, Tap, Tap =
Tap, Tap—Tap, Tap, Tap, Tap =
Tap, Tap, Tap—Tap, Tap, Tap =

Tap, Tap, Tap, Tap—Tap, Tap, Tap, Tap, Tap =
Tap, Tap, Tap—Tap, Tap, Tap, Tap, Tap =

Tap, Tap—Tap =
Tap, Tap, Tap, Tap—Tap, Tap, Tap =
Tap—Tap, Tap, Tap, Tap, Tap =
Tap—Tap, Tap, Tap, Tap, Tap =
Tap—Tap, Tap, Tap, Tap =
Tap, Tap, Tap—Tap, Tap, Tap, Tap, Tap =
Tap, Tap, Tap—Tap, Tap, Tap =

QUIZ 4

In order to solve codes and ciphers, a good cryptanalyst has to know how to create them too. Here you must apply the Cyrillic alphabet and the quadrilateral method. To send a message containing the letters at the left, decide the number of taps needed on both sides of the pause (—). For example, to send *o*, the tap numbers would be *three* (for the letter group)—*four* (for the letter's position in the group). (Answers on page 256.)

1.   Ш ш   _____ — _____

2.   Р р   _____ — _____

3.   Д д   _____ — _____

4.   Э э   _____ — _____

5.   П п   _____ — _____

6.   Ж ж   _____ — _____

7.   Ю ю   _____ — _____

8.   Г г   _____ — _____

9.   Н н   _____ — _____

10.   Ф ф   _____ — _____

QUIZ 5

Here in the chamber, more of the long-held secrets of the Rosicrucians can be found. Apply what you learned about them in Chapter 7 to determine the names of these wise people. (Answers on page 256.)

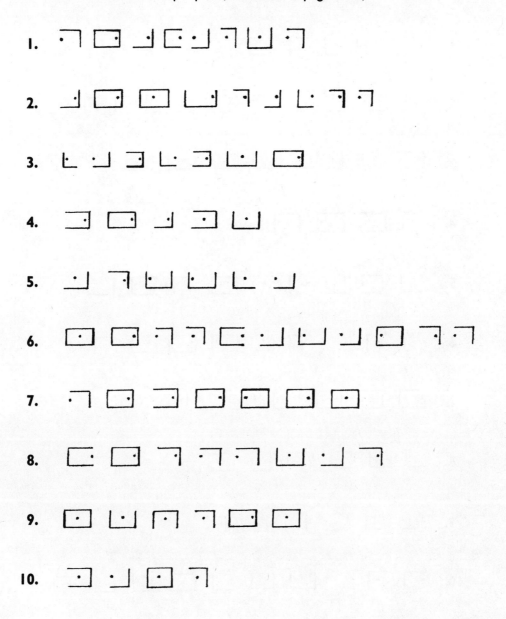

QUIZ 6

The Rosicrucians sought a balance of religion, science, and philosophy for mankind's betterment. Continue to seek the truth in the names hidden below. (Answers on page 256.)

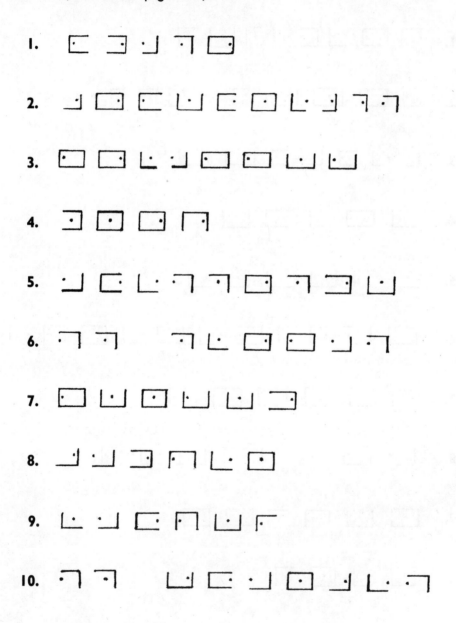

QUIZ 7

The Masons have had a number of United States presidents as members. First discern the meaning of the Mason's ciphers. Then name the president with whom the decipherment is best associated. (Answers on page 256.)

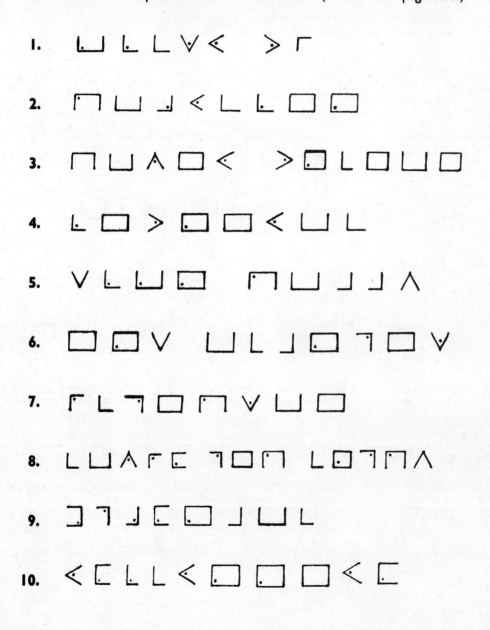

QUIZ 8

The list of American presidents and the Mason's ciphers containing clues to their identities continues. (Answers on page 256.)

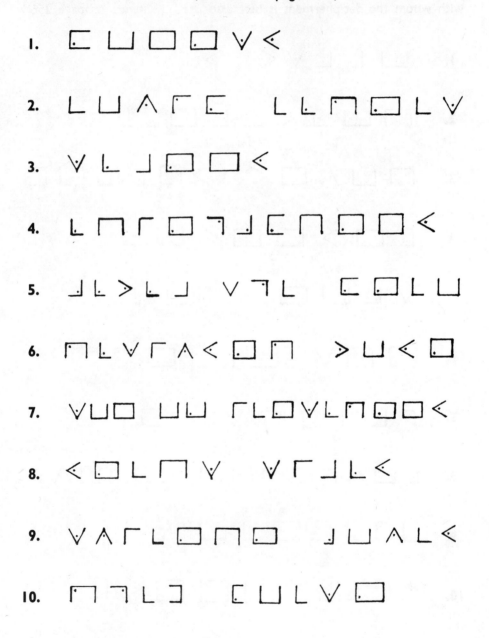

QUIZ 9

Use the one-handed alphabet of Abbé Charles de l'Épée to learn about words that he used and that are so important today. (Answers on page 256.)

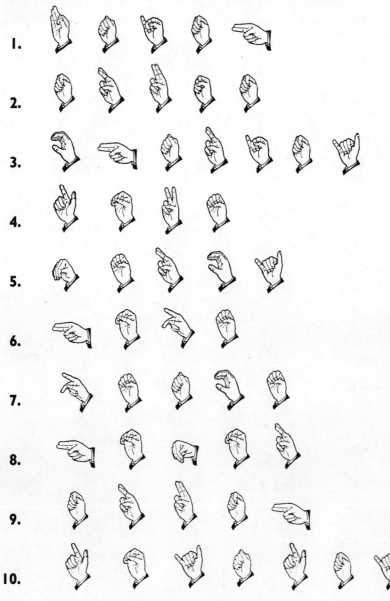

QUIZ 10

Many people learned to count on their fingers in the time of Abbé de l'Épée. One's fingers are still quite "handy" even in the modern calculator age. Here is a collection of digits ready for deciphering. (Answers on page 256.)

1. × − + = _____

2. + × − = _____

3. ÷ × + = _____

4. × + − = _____

5. + − × = _____

6. ÷ + × = _____

7. × + ÷ = _____

8. × − + = _____

9. + × ÷ = _____

10. − + × = _____

III.

EMPERORS

AND

EMPIRE

8

YANKEE DOODLE'S DAY

$\twoheadleftarrow\!\!\leftarrow\!\!\leftarrow$

Valley Forge. It might not have been a hallowed name in the American Revolutionary War if one woman had not had a very sharp sense of hearing. That careful listener was the rarely mentioned Quaker heroine, Lydia Darragh. Very few facts about her personal life were preserved, aside from her letters, but if she had not noticed what can logically be called an unusual code of sounds, the cause of Colonial liberty could very easily have been lost.

Darragh was a midwife and nurse in Philadelphia. During the crucial winter of 1777, British Gen. Sir William Howe was requisitioning lodgings and central locations for quartering and positioning his troops. He used his authority to commandeer Lydia and William Darraghs' home for a meeting place.

The possibility of eviction was compounded by a second factor. Their eldest son Charles had disobeyed them and joined the nearby rebel army. Though he had broken the vows of the Society of Friends, they still loved him. Constantly worried about their son, the Darraghs naturally were curious about Howe's intentions.

A devout Quaker and pacifist, Lydia Darragh was faced with a dilemma. Should she try to help the Continental army, or should she retain her neutrality? She decided to help the rebels, and by extension, her son and the new country.

Whenever she had the chance, Darragh began the risk of learning more. Carefully becoming familiar with the uninvited officers, she was eventually able to find out about their personal traits and habits. By direct and indirect eavesdropping, she also noticed an unusual pattern of behavior. If these men had actual orders to go on patrols or to maneuver their troops, they gave audible indications of the impending actions. One fellow's habit of rocking on his wing-backed chair and another's of drumming his fingers on a tabletop became a kind of aural code for Darragh.

On December 2, 1777, these telltale sounds were accompanied by an extra number of adjutants arriving and departing. These harbingers of activity made Darragh boldly listen by a cupboard wall. She was shocked to learn that General Howe himself had given the command for a surprise attack on Washington's army: it was to begin the night of December 4.

By the morning of the 4th Darragh had formulated a brave plan unknown even to her husband. She pretended to need flour from a mill near Whitemarsh, one of the colonial army's outposts. Along the way to the Frankford grindstones, she quietly met with rebel Col. Thomas Craig, who was a trusted friend. After relating what she knew, she got the flour and returned home.

Thus alerted, General Washington was able to bolster his defenses. On the evening of December 4 Howe's forces did open fire on some Colonial units at Chestnut Hill near Whitemarsh. But they were stunned by vollies of return shots that sent them running for cover. The redcoats' element of surprise and some of their number were lost in the snowswept fields that night. Thanks to Lydia Darragh and the man who heeded her warning, the Colonial army was saved to continue the struggle for freedom.

A much better known resident of Philadelphia helped popularize an unusual kind of puzzle consisting of words, symbols, and figures. The man was Benjamin Franklin and his codelike writing was called a *rebus.* Yet, creative as he was, he did not originate it.

Rebuses were known in ancient times. The word *rebus* is believed to have originated with the Latin word *res,* the ablative plural for *thing.* The literal meaning of the word was *by things* because the sounds of the figures and symbols combine to create a complete phrase.

The rebus was used in England in the Middle Ages in the form of brief pictoral imagery in signatures. Rebuses were also applied as decorations on important papers like deeds and birth records. In heraldry they were used as parts of coats of arms depicting family names.

Foxman   Heartwell   Waterson (sun)

The uses for rebuses were expanded in France during the 1500s. In the provinces, carnivals and pageants often included performances that incorporated symbolic puzzles. These satirized everything from local life to the national government. The shows in one particular region, Picardy, were so popular that they came to be titled *rebus de Picardie.*

With his extensive knowledge of France and his fascination for the unusual, it is not surprising that Franklin would have been amused by rebuses and applied them in his writing. It might be surmised that Franklin's droll humor could also have been serving to conceal messages in other seemingly innocent figures. To some his drawing of a teapot could have been a reference to the Boston Tea Party. This in turn might have been a coded link to the Sons of Liberty, one of the earliest anti-Royalist groups in the colonies.

Franklin used ciphers in situations that called for serious concealment. When he had the crucial and influential role of special ambassador to France, he protected several of his communications with letter substitutions.

The British employed a number of concealment methods in their efforts to counteract the rebellion. England's agents exchanged communications by several means, including hollow quill pens, hidden pockets, and false-bottomed boxes. One interesting type of device used by Gen. Sir Henry Clinton was what he and his associates called a *mask.* Actually a kind of grille, it involved a plaintext message filled with extraneous words, and sheets of paper with shapes cut in them. Though obviously not foolproof, this method was chosen by Clinton for his important exchanges with Gen. John Burgoyne in 1777. Their correspondence was linked to Burgoyne's invasion from Canada through the Lake Champlain region and into the Hudson Valley.

Here are the contents of one of these letters, dated August 10, 1777.

The real message was to be found within the hourglass likeness representing a cutout in the covering paper:

```
You will have heard, Dr Sir I doubt not long before this
can have reached you that Sir W. Howe is gone from hence. The
Rebels imagine that he is gone to the Southward. By this time
however he has filled Chesapeak bay with surprize and terror.
   Washington marched the greatest part of the Rebels to Philadelphia
in order to oppose Sir Wms army. I hear he is now returned upon
finding none of our troops landed but am not sure of this great part
of his troops are returned for certain I am sure this (illegible)
must be vain to them. I am left to command here, half my force may
I am sure defend every thing here with as much safety I shall therefore
send Sir W. 4 or 5 batn I have too small a force to invade the New England
provinces, they are too weak to make any effectual efforts against me and
you do not want any diversion in your favour I can therefore very well
spare him 1500 men. I shall try something certainly towards the close
of the year not till then at any rate. It may be of use to inform you that
report says all yields to you. I own to you that the business will
quickly be over now. Sr W's move just at this time has been Capital
Washingtons have been the worst he could take in every respect I
sincerely give you much joy on your success and am with great
sincerity. . . .
```

At the time of this letter, neither general could foresee the fateful days of October 1777. During a series of confrontations in the battle of Saratoga, Burgoyne's army was soundly defeated. This rebel victory sent a shock wave through the royal courts of Europe. Colonial Gen. Horatio Gates was given credit as overall commander. Yet many observers believed that a heroic charge led by Benedict Arnold helped save the day. Theorists have since speculated that Arnold's not receiving proper credit helped lead to his eventual shift in loyalty.

Perhaps the best-known case of treason in American history, the infamous actions of Arnold also involved codes. This moody, volatile man must have felt badly slighted after helping defeat Burgoyne. Records of those times indicate that he was very disturbed by rewards and promotions granted to others on different occasions as well. When he let greed exacerbate his wounded pride, he chose to turn on the patriot cause. His plan to compromise the strategic West Point fort is well known. His use of codes to send messages to his coconspirators is much less frequently documented. Yet Arnold nearly succeeded, and an awkward but involved type of code helped.

Arnold's military counterpart in the British army was Maj. John André. André was a young, cultured gentleman whose sole motive in the plot seemed to have been loyalty to the crown. Apparently Arnold performed his own encoding duties. The redcoats' cryptologists were Jonathan Odell, a New York pastor, and a Philadelphia merchant named Joseph Stansbury.

The plotters used book codes. This method involved a prearranged text that provided words and phrases from its contents. Both message sender and recipient had identical copies of the chosen book to avoid confusion.

They used as a basis the first volume of Oxford's fifth edition of Blackstone's *Commentaries*. They used three numbers to make each word. The first number represented the page, the second the line, and the third the word (e.g., 34.15.8). Those words that could not be found in the book had to be spelled out. They began to have problems when important words used in military parlance could not be found whole. Matters became further complicated when they had to mix increasing amounts of spelled and numbered phrases. Arnold chose to discard this system after learning that Stansbury and Odell were having difficulty with the long, involved cryptograms.

The plotters decided to change to the lexicon of one Nathan Bailey, the *Universal Etymological English Dictionary*. Because its words were arranged alphabetically, they were much easier to find. However, for some reason not recorded by researchers, they again shifted their code base to an unidentified dictionary. With it they used a three-part number foundation of page, column, and word. They also began enciphering their new code numbers with the addition of 7 to each of the three groups. Oddly, in so doing, they created a rather simple giveaway to breaking their system. Can you guess what repetitious pattern they made by always adding 7? Let us move away from history for a moment to consider this flaw.

Previously, their Blackstone book code was arranged by the page, line, and then the word. For example, 50.1.10 would represent page fifty, line one, and word ten. The use of dictionaries involved exchanging lines for columns. Yet while the columns were neatly arranged, the plotters' system limited them to being numbered 1 or 2. But by adding 7 (1 + 7 and 2 + 7), the columns always appeared as 8 or 9 in the code. Any cryptanalyst worth his or her proverbial salt would have noticed this. Ironically, no rebel codebreaker ever got a chance to do so.

Because of the trust and respect that Arnold had previously achieved, he was not being watched nor was his correspondence being studied.

Not a single one of his missives was ever intercepted for analysis. Thus, the actual strength of the code was never tested. Rather, it was the capture of André by a wary rebel patrol that foiled the nearly successful conspiracy. The British major had no code that could help him avoid the hangman's noose. Arnold fled to England and lived to see his once proud name forever tarnished.

The near disastrous loss of the vital Hudson fortress caused General Washington and other Colonial leaders to urge an increase in code-making and spying efforts on every front. One of the sites where the rebels could count on efficiency was in a rather unusual place, Loyalist-dominated New York City.

Three of the best rebel agent/codemakers were residing in that area: Maj. Benjamin Tallmadge, originally of the Second Connecticut Dragoons, New York's own Robert Townsend, and Samuel Woodhull of Setauket, Long Island. Townsend was given the code name Culper Junior while Woodhull was Culper Senior. These three men and their friends had the unenviable task of gathering information in a city that the redcoats had turned into a virtual armed camp. Since the British did have a number of supporters there, it was difficult for Tallmadge and the Culpers to send messages by visual signals such as lanterns or objects mounted in doors and windows. A written code that could be transferred by courier, rider, and oarsman was crucial. It was Major Tallmadge who chose a book code for them from the *New Spelling Dictionary* by John Entick. After writing selected words in a column, he gave each word a number. The names of specific locations and people were placed in a separate part of the code. Some examples include: 356 = letter, 660 = vigilant, 711 = George Washington, 727 = New York. Additionally, a type of mixed alphabet served to form words not easily categorized on the main list. It was set up as follows:

```
a b c d e f g h i j k l m n o p q r s t u v w x y z
─────────────────────────────────────────────────────
e f g h i j a b c d o m n p q r k l u v w x y z s t
```

To shield their reports further, the spies used invisible inks, which they called *stains*. Some were made from lemon and onion juice applied with quills to parchment. To the average eye, the words written with this base were invisible. They were "developed" at Washington's headquarters by holding the letters above a source of heat. The added temperature revealed the hidden and encoded words. Different and very effective stains created by John Jay's physician brother, Sir James Jay, were so secret that their chemical makeup was never revealed.

The combination of the Entick code and the invisible inks enabled the rebel agents to compile valuable facts (after painstaking efforts). Information about British troop strength, morale, supplies, and even Royal Navy ships in the harbor was valuable.

General Washington was able to learn much about the preferences and inclinations of his Loyalist rival Gen. Henry Clinton. By this time Clinton commanded the British war effort from his base in the New York garrison. By carefully moving his own troops into key positions around the city, the Virginia squire kept Clinton off guard. Though he had a much more powerful force, Clinton dared not lose the key port with its harbor for the navy. Thus, Clinton ended up on the defensive, and his men often came under sniper fire when they wandered too far from the city proper.

A great deal of conjecture exists among military analysts regarding Clinton's inaction. Many have offered examples of how he could have successfully moved against the thin arc of Colonial troops around the city on a number of occasions. However, hindsight in warfare is always much clearer than the vision afforded to anyone using a long glass to peer at woods or shores on the eve of battle. What is certain is that George Washington was clever enough to turn a very tenuous defensive position into a virtual stalemate. He developed a spy/code system and was not too vain to heed the knowledge it generated.

The New York "draw" was thus brought about with the help of a dictionary-based code. The standoff in this region was to prove doubly important as events unfolded in the southern colonies. Because Washington kept the pressure on Clinton, the British commander could not move his formidable garrison at will. Nor could he quickly send large numbers of reinforcements to the hard-pressed redcoats in the South.

By autumn of 1781, English Gen. Charles Cornwallis had chosen a Virginia coastal site, Yorktown, as a base of operations. Hoping to receive Royal Navy support from the sea-lanes to New York, he was instead hemmed in by a Colonial army led by Nathaniel Greene and the Marquis de Lafayette. In a strategically brilliant decision, Washington cleverly pretended to continue encircling New York. In fact, he took the majority of his forces to join Lafayette and Greene. Fooled by Washington, Clinton held his reserves too long in New York. The besieged Cornwallis was forced to surrender on October 17.

On that historic day, different accounts indicate that one or more bands played an old English air. Some knew it as the song called "When the King Enjoys His Own Again." But others were certain that they recognized the tune "The World Turn'd Upside Down." Surely the world's monarchies were stunned by the news emanating from the Virginia seaside village.

9

SEAFARING SIGNALS

{{{{

rom the days of the Phoenicians and the Vikings to present-day
fleets, sailors have communicated by ingenious methods. The men
who charted their courses by the stars knew as much about the
importance of signals and codes as did their land-dwelling counterparts.

Records of marine communications and secrecy devices were not
well kept before 1530. That year is noted by naval historians for two
reasons. The first involves a Spanish writer, Alonso de Chaves, who
happened to mention Spain's navy in some of his passages. In one he
wrote about the use of a distinctive signaling system. However, the
details of this method were not listed.

This omission and the lack of records in general may have had a
rather simple explanation. None of the great seafaring nations had
standardized their signals on paper at this time, let alone chiseled them
on tablets. Proud captains gave their own signs and the varied meanings
to a few trusted subordinates. Any man depending on a book to make
his plans would have been tossed overboard if not keelhauled.

The year 1530 is also relevant because of an event recorded by the
ocean-conscious British. That year someone in the English naval hierarchy issued a command for admirals' vessels. Such ships were ordered
to raise a recognizable flag to their masthead. These banners were to
be standardized, and deference was to be paid to them by every
supporting craft. It is believed that this decision set the pattern of a
command vessel, the flagship.

The historic defeat of the Spanish Armada led to Great Britain's rise
to naval predominance. With this power came the explorers who sought
new worlds. Among them was the courtier and adventurer Sir Walter
Raleigh. Because Raleigh was interested in New World settlements, he
helped finance and direct expeditions. Raleigh is credited with compiling

the first set of signal directions for use between vessels. By a combination of raised and lowered sails and audible gunfire or cannon shots, he conveyed his intentions to other captains and crews.

With the exploration of the territories named the Americas and the discovery of unimagined mineral wealth, another kind of danger spread over the seas: pirates. Thriving in Caribbean coves and hundreds of mainland inlets, these buccaneers had their own signals and visual codes. Whether operating alone or in pairs, they used switched flags, waving lanterns, and faked fires to trick the gold-laden convoys and their armed escorts.

Half a century after the infamy of Blackbeard and Anne Bonny, another type of naval raider gained favor in Colonial America. These men were called *privateers,* and their daring efforts against the extremely powerful British squadrons were necessary for the survival of the rebellion. As their name implies, their vessels were privately owned. Eventually, these vessels and their captains proved crucial in gaining the victory.

Shipowners first applied for a privateering commission and Letters of Marque from a Colonial governor. The governors had vice-admiralty powers in wartime. The Letters of Marque were similar to licenses. They authorized the arming of a vessel for the purpose of capturing the ships and property of an enemy nation. Within about one year (in April 1776) the Continental Congress started to grant these commissions as well. After a time the Congress became the sole purveyor of the credentials.

From the outset of the conflict, these oceanic rebels kept vital supply links open. Quietly but steadily they provided everything from powder and shot to salt. The latter was not just a condiment; it was a very necessary preservative without which farm wives, city dwellers, and Washington's valiant army could have starved. The salt was not merely carried along Colonial rivers. It came from distant Caribbean islands by a very dangerous route. Between high winds, unseen shoals, and British cannons, many craft never returned to home port. Yet those that did compiled quite an impressive record. They accounted for the following losses suffered by King George's navy: sixteen warships, more than two-thousand nine-hundred Royalist merchantmen, and captured goods with a combined value of nearly fifty-million dollars.

The owners of the ships had taken risks and thus received their share of the profits from capture. Still, numerous benefits accrued to the

Congress and the widely dispersed rebel factions from New England to Georgia. While historians correctly note the importance of the French alliance, they often overlook these bold defenders of our waterways.

Having briefly described such contributions, let's take a closer look at the ways in which the privateers outwitted the skilled British navy. Certainly the colonists had experienced seamen. The whaling men of New Bedford and other such coastal ports were considered to be some of the finest afloat. Yet it took painstakingly coordinated plans as well as more than a little luck to outwit King George's admirals.

As previously mentioned, ships carried a number of national flags, sometimes a whole trunkful. Switching banners to trick a foe was considered an acceptable *ruse de guerre*. When two rebel vessels used this scheme on each other, however, the potential losses often outweighed the gains. Therefore, as the war continued and increasing numbers of Colonial ships operated in pairs or groups, more effective flag and lantern codes were developed.

If the commanding officer wanted to give an order for "full sail with first wind," he would place a European flag at the peak of his ship's mainmast:

If the enemy were sighted and the commander wished to pursue, he would order "begin chase" by placing an English ensign on the ensign staff at his vessel's stern. Also, he would hoist a pennant to his foretopgallant masthead:

The command to "begin engaging the enemy" could be given by lowering the English ensign from its staff and raising a European flag in its place:

When actually ready to fire opening salvos, captains proudly raised the flag of their own colony. At this point no secrets were being kept or surprises being planned. However, at night, when flags were not appropriate, lanterns were also used.

Should a seaman in a crow's-nest spot an unfamiliar sail configuration or a possible enemy vessel, he would report this. Other friendly privateers might then be notified. A flag or a pennant might not be used because such an action could be noticed by an alert enemy with a long glass. Instead, a lantern would be raised at the ensign staff, then lowered and raised again in a preset signal pattern. Certainly this light could be observed at night. To reduce the chances of detection, canvas was used to shroud the brightness:

Battles at times of poor visibility required light signals as well. According to previous arrangements, lanterns hung fore and aft or along the rail in alignment with different masts were signs that friends were near:

A formalized version of lantern signals was developed and applied by the English admiral Baron George Rodney in the early 1780s. Once seen, such a system was eventually "borrowed" and altered by the privateers to suit their own purposes. Instead of a single light or randomly placed lanterns, the Rodney approach used clusters of lanterns mounted by ropes and attached to yardarms in a hoist apparatus:

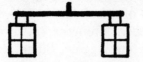

Such lantern systems would have been a logical progression for night use, based not only on convenience but also safety when used near powder and pine-tar stores. Still, as far into the century as the year 1826, a Frenchman created a system combining flags by day, torches by night, and cannons for inclement weather. Le Comte Missiessy incorporated time intervals while communicating at anchor or under sail. His torch version indicated numbers with a base sequence of one to five, then a timed pause, followed by different additions of torches according to a set pattern:

3 = ψ ψ ψ

8 = ψ ψ ψ -- ψ

14 = ψ ψ ψ ψ -- ψ ψ

Flags on halyards and a kind of human signal method were united in the 1850s with a system designed by Capt. Charles de Reynold-Chauvancy. Popularly called the *Reynold's code,* it had a resourceful distress signal system whereby a man could use a pole and even his hat to convey numerals:

1 =

7 =

9 =

The lessons taught by Americans John Paul Jones in the Atlantic and Oliver Hazard Perry on Lake Erie a generation later remained all too fresh in the minds of the British. They realized that their own chain of command needed strengthening from the position of fleet admiral to the sailor in the rigging. Since communications were the figurative "mainsails" of this policy, the reorganization of all signal systems and code/ciphers was given high priority.

Actually, an English rear admiral had compiled a type of alphabetized flag code as early as 1803. Sir Home Popham was the man credited with making such a structured linkup of banners and a code. But previous to the naval setbacks of 1812 Popham's efforts had not been appreciated. In the postwar search for improvements, his work was reconsidered. Heartened by this renewed interest, Popham improved his code with a series of numerical flags. His combinations of three and four flags led to an expanded vocabulary of 30,000 words.

Another imaginative individual whose efforts paralleled those of Popham was Frederick Marryat, captain of the Royal Navy. An author of novels such as *Jacob Faithful* and *Mr. Midshipman Easy,* Marryat had also published the *Code of Signals for the Merchant Service* in 1817.

Military-service competition and business rivalries kept flag-hoist uniformity from being accepted. As the decades passed, debates over color, banner shape, pennant size, and so forth continued.

England's signal indecision was mirrored in the actions of other major naval powers like France and Italy. With each of these countries attempting to develop its own military and merchant fleet signals, it is no wonder that mass confusion resulted.

Since the most practical use of the open seas required cooperation between noncombatants, the need for mutually understood flag-hoist signals became widespread. While lanterns, lamps, whistles, and horns were mainly relegated to a position of night and fog warning mechanisms, flags maintained their primary role for day signals.

In 1857 one of the better attempts at formulating a universal maritime communication system was made by the British Board of Trade. That year they decided upon a standard system of eighteen colored flags. These banners, which represented all the consonants except *x* and *z,* were to be used openly by English merchant vessels. Combinations of these banners provided a code of some 70,000 signals, which were published in a text entitled *The Commercial Code of Signals.* Not to be outdone by their frequent rivals, the French responded the next year with their *Code Commercial des Signaux.* Nevertheless, disagreements continued between these two nations and among others regarding these signals.

While the debate wore on, almost every naval authority and advocate agreed that safety was of paramount importance. One of the more unusual and serviceable devices for safety and secrecy was introduced in the 1870s. Invented by a Maine native, it was a type of signal means known as *pyrotechnic* (Greek: *pyros,* a fire + *technē,* art).

Edward Very was the Down Easter who developed the method that bears his name. Born in 1845, Very served in the navy in the Civil War. Later, at the Washington Navy Yard, he began ordnance experiments. In 1877 he introduced a code for day and night messages. A year later he patented a signal cartridge to bring his own paper code "to light."

Very's invention was similar to a Roman candle. The exploding message "stars" were launched from a single-shot pistol to a height of approximately two-hundred feet. The powder "stars" were encased in brass shells. They burned green, red, or white in color for use in darkness. In daylight hours another type of shell produced a trail of smoke. The code simply used a pattern of alphabet letters and corresponding number (1–26) positions. Thus, *a* = 1 star shot. When numbers were needed, a color variation was used to indicate that those numbers would be next. Then 0 through 9 could be represented and not be confused with letters. Extra bursts or color changes could be added to represent nulls and mask the communication.

The *Very Light,* as it was called, brought some order, especially to night signaling, through pyrotechnics, yet no one method stabilized the flag-hoist situation. Only over the course of many years did the nations of the world finally arrive at an international maritime standard. Had the decisions been made by sailors, the alphabet chart represented here might have been created much earlier:

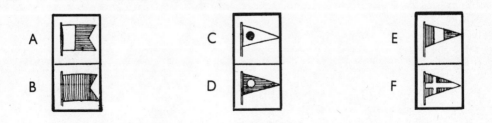

G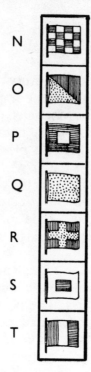

H

I

J

K

L

M

N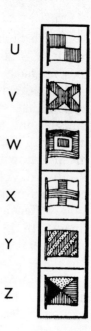

O

P

Q

R

S

T

U

V

W

X

Y

Z

10

CROWN, CONSPIRACY, CORSICAN

‹‹‹‹

America had won her independence, and the word *revolution* was no longer limited to banned books or the theories of obscure philosophers. America's example had a crucial effect on her wartime ally, France.

While both enlightened and self-serving in helping America, France herself was in a state of ever-deepening social and economic strife. Years of royal excesses had led to an extremely volatile situation. The formerly wise and well-advised Bourbon dynasty was, by the 1780s, in the questionable hands of Louis XVI.

No credible historian has ever proved that Louis was an evil man. Rather, he suffered from the ills of those who inherit a throne on the basis of kinship alone. He was plagued by almost every kingly malady, from indifference to ignorance of the military chain of command. His bride, Marie Antoinette, did not help matters, as she lived as if the idea of "no tomorrow" were a self-fulfilling prophecy.

Marie is usually depicted as a giddy, flirtatious spendthrift, yet there are those who contend that she should not be faulted for trying to live the only kind of life she knew. Her parents and husband were much more to blame for her behavior since they should have guided and advised her. Instead, she had to face the intrigues and back-stabbing jealousies of the increasingly decadent Versailles court.

Retreating from public life, she angered Louis. She mistakenly let herself be surrounded by the type of sycophants who were adept at befriending lonely, disillusioned people. Marie's spending binges and disputes with Louis were cleverly encouraged by her entourage. They benefited both by her shared opulence and by being at the very center of royal influence.

During times of increased alienation, both Louis and Marie had affairs. One of Marie's relationships is of interest here because it involved both enciphered love letters and political intrigues. Her secret paramour was Hans Axel Fersen, a Swedish count who had helped in the American Colonials' revolt.

It is conceivable that the queen's mother, Empress Maria Theresa, influenced Marie with her own knowledge of secret missives. It is possible that Marie might have heard talk of nomenclators or Vigenère tableaus around the Austrian palaces. A quiet visit to one of Maria Theresa's many rooms might have led to the discovery of a cipher alphabet in an unlocked drawer. Whatever the source, the young queen had enough knowledge and ability not to falter.

Though Louis XVI and Marie Antoinette were divided in their personal lives, the year 1789 brought a national crisis to the doors of Versailles. France's long-festering ills became a national fever called revolution. The storming of the Bastille was more symbolic than dangerous to the monarchy, but the sacking of estates, the disloyalty of army units, and the murders of numerous aristocrats were clear signs of serious political trouble.

Louis XVI seemed to flounder after he and Marie had to leave Versailles. They were escorted to the Tuileries palace in Paris, supposedly for their safety. Yet while Louis became more confused and ineffective, Marie demonstrated an inner resolve that surprised her critics.

In a curious linkage of personal relationships, it was she and Count Fersen who used ciphers to exchange plans with loyal monarchists. She and Fersen hoped to unite the numerous but disorganized provincials who still held the royal family in awe. It was Fersen, with his war experience, who took care of the clandestine meetings with their followers.

These ciphers had key words. Their letters were located in groups aligned vertically. The plain and ciphered letters were arranged horizontally beside the capitals in a way similar to the example here:

```
H   m o   p r   s u   v x   y a   b d   e g   h j
I   a b   c d   e f   g h   i j   k l   m n   o p
J   k n   o r   s v   w z   a d   e h   i l   m p
K   c g   h l   m q   r v   w a   b f   g k   l p
L   a x   b y   c z   d a   e b   f c   g d   h e
```

When Fersen or Marie sent a rather simple missive, they might use key letter I. In this version the plaintext letter c became enciphered d. The word `aim` would be enciphered as `bjn`. However, key J would cause *aim* to become `dlp`. Each key provided a different encipherment pattern.

Though this multiple alphabet did not compare to other types in difficulty, it was enough to fool the increasingly violent Paris mobs. The leaders of various factions, including Danton and Robespierre, were too busy trying to consolidate their own shaky positions among the many shifting allegiances to be able to watch the Royalists' every move. Nor were there men of the caliber of Rossignol who could be hired to seek and break codes.

Louis and Marie did hire Honoré Gabriel Mirabeau, a popular orator, in an attempt to steer the nation toward a constitutional monarchy. However, when Mirabeau died in 1791 and the threats to their personal safety increased, the queen persuaded the king to flee to France's eastern provinces.

A rather elaborate scheme was arranged for the couple and their children to appear to be retiring for the evening at the Tuileries. Instead, they pretended to be servants and began their departure in an enclosed carriage. Count Fersen remained loyal and was disguised as their driver. They hoped to meet supporters near the border, and indeed they seemed to have their goal within reach. But the distance across a small bridge was to prove very long indeed. In the village of Varennes a local man's wagon happened to block access to the entrance of the bridge at a most inopportune time. The family was recognized and their journey was abruptly halted. They were placed under virtual arrest and returned to Paris. Count Fersen managed to avoid punishment and continued to remain a Royalist, though separated from the queen.

More purposeful than ever before, Marie sought help from others. She encouraged her brother, Leopold II of Austria, to challenge the Jacobin revolutionaries. In more secret correspondence, she sought a union of other royal houses against the spread of radicalism. Even while Louis agreed to abide by a new constitution formulated by moderates, the queen remained in touch with other governments. Desperate, Louis acquiesced in these actions. Marie's attempts were nearly successful when a confrontation between France and Austria seemed imminent in 1792. Hoping to guarantee the defeat of the rebels' forces, she took the fateful step of divulging the French army's plans to her friends in Vienna.

An outbreak of renewed fighting within France toppled the constitutional monarchy in August 1792. The moderates lost any foundations of legitimacy they might have had. Leopold's threats faltered and the Jacobins gained full control. These hardcore rebels wanted revenge for years of real grievances, but they soon were corrupted by their power and turned France over to the mob rule of what became known as the Reign of Terror.

By this time the royal family's complicity with other monarchs was made known. Their attempts led to accusations of counterrevolutionary plots. Because the Jacobins and their friends were now the reigning government, they charged Marie and Louis with treason.

Almost eight months to the day after the king's execution, on January 21, 1793, Marie was found guilty of secret intrigues with foreign powers. Much like Mary, Queen of Scots, Marie's use of ciphers had led to her downfall. Strangely, though, had she and Fersen not been so successful in reaching other royalty, the treason charges may not have been taken seriously. Not at all the giddy "Madame Deficit," Marie Antoinette was also very similar to Mary, Queen of Scots in dignity when she was executed at the guillotine.

As for Count Fersen, he returned to his native Sweden, deeply saddened by Marie's death. Not much more is known about his last years. Fersen's life ended in 1810 because of a tragic misconception. Falsely charged with poisoning Sweden's crown prince, he was murdered by a Stockholm mob.

As the 1700s drew to a close, not only a cipher advance but also a strange conspiracy occurred in America. Though separate events, they were linked by the odd relationship of the men responsible for them.

Though inventiveness is often associated with Benjamin Franklin during this era, it was another famous colonist who devised a worthy code-related creation. The man was Thomas Jefferson, and he developed what he called a *wheel cypher*. Improved by him during the years 1790 to 1800, his invention looked something like this:

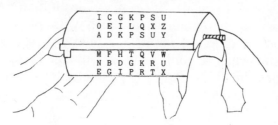

Measuring six inches long by two inches wide, the device was convenient to use. Furthermore, its central shaft held thirty-six wheels (disks), and twenty-six letters formed on their outer edges. With a key or other arrangement, these disks would be set to align the letters of the desired plaintext sequence. Then any one of the other letter lines could be sent as the ciphertext. The recipient would first align these jumbled letters with his device. This would cause his wheels to be arranged so as to reveal the desired plaintext at another point along the row of disks. Additional variety was gained by altering the positions of the wheels on the shaft.

This device was well ahead of its time. In fact, it superseded a number of creative attempts in Europe. Yet neither the United States military nor the fledgling diplomatic corps was to benefit from the wheel cypher because Thomas Jefferson did not apply it for practical use. Occupied with his many activities and presidential responsibilities, he put it aside. Not until one hundred twenty or so years later was a similar version of the wheel cypher made available to United States armed forces. Yet its inherent worth is verified by the fact that the American navy made use of such a mechanism for decades after its introduction.

While Jefferson's many interests may not have permitted him to concentrate on cipher making/breaking, it should be said that he had no need to protect most aspects of his very open presidency. Yet the unscrupulous politician/adventurer who had been as close to his office as the vice-presidency was eventually revealed to have used a combination of codes and ciphers in dealings that led to a treason case. The man was Aaron Burr, and he came within one Electoral College vote of being our third president.

Born in 1756, Burr matured during the tumultuous early years of America. He secured command of a Colonial regiment in 1777 and fought bravely in the Battle of Monmouth a year later. He even served for a time on Benedict Arnold's staff. Burr was no longer associated with Arnold during his West Point treason plan. However, this service with Arnold did bring Burr into contact with another young officer named James Wilkinson, who was to be involved directly with Burr at a later date.

In busy postwar New York, Burr became a lawyer with political organizing skills and a polished style. He turned the city's Tammany Social Club into one of the first American vote "machines." This led to a strong position in the New York State legislature and eventual control of the presidential electoral votes for New York.

Realizing his influence, the Jeffersonian Republicans picked him to be Thomas Jefferson's vice-president in 1796 and 1800. The first time on the ballot, Burr finished third. But in 1800 the variables of the Electoral College led to an unusual situation. The electors cast an equal number of votes—seventy-three—for each man, compared to sixty-three for Federalist rival John Adams. Thus, the election had to be settled by the House of Representatives.

Because Jefferson's backers were also the party's leaders, they did not look favorably upon Burr's sudden prominence. Though Jefferson did not personally compete with Burr, history indicates that he followed his advisers' words to place some distance between himself and the fast-rising New Jersey native. As the House started deliberating, Burr began to feel this alienation.

However, the crushing blow to Burr's presidential hopes came not from the Jeffersonians but from his New York political rival Alexander Hamilton. After a week of House indecision and thirty-five ballots, Hamilton persuaded some of his New York associates to cast blank ballots. Jefferson's men held firm, repeated their votes on the thirty-sixth ballot, and rejoiced when their candidate was declared president.

Burr continued this term as vice president though he was understandably disillusioned. By 1804 his seething bitterness was a prime factor in his seeking a stronger political base. To do so, he entered New York's gubernatorial race with private Federalist backing. At the same time some New England Federalists, with names like the "Essex Junto" and the "River Gods," were so upset with Jefferson's policies that they seriously considered forming a New England–New York confederacy.

Hamilton learned of this plan, publicly linked Burr with it, and angrily denounced the idea as a nation-weakening plot. These accusations effectively destroyed Burr's support in upstate New York and thus cost him the governorship. Enraged by Hamilton's actions, Burr challenged him to a duel. On July 11, 1804, the pistol exchange at Weehawken, New Jersey, ended with Hamilton being mortally wounded. But in gaining what he considered to be a gentleman's revenge, Burr had begun to sound the death knell for his political career.

Hamilton's death caused a public outcry that Burr could not have envisioned. Even many of his closest Tammany friends turned against him. He reacted by creating one of the oddest schemes in American history. Reports about his complicated plot included foreign money, a private army, territorial acquisitions, and ciphers to link the grandiose venture.

Various sources tried to connect his monetary support to British and Spanish interests who sought a breakup of the recently united colonies. Amounts of as much as half a million dollars had been heard when other rumors mounted that Burr dreamed of his own empire in the Western territories. No doubt his links to the failed New England confederacy fueled this speculation.

Burr did resume his association with James Wilkinson, now a general in charge of the newly acquired Louisiana Territory. With funds apparently supplied by his son-in-law, Joseph Alston, and by a wealthy Irishman named Harman Blennerhassett, Burr purchased title to more than a million acres of Orleans Territory. Burr also had a strategic base of operations on an Ohio River island owned by Blennerhassett. From this site in 1806 Burr sent messages to Wilkinson in a combination dictionary code and symbol cipher. In the late summer of that same year he left Blennerhassett's island with sixty men on thirteen flatboats.

Unknown to Burr, James Wilkinson sent one of the deciphered copies of their missives to Washington, D.C. It was quickly taken to President Jefferson's office. Upon reading it, the man who had once shared the Republican ballot with Burr now ordered the suspected expedition to be disbanded and Burr to be arrested. After some months, Burr was caught. His mysterious plans halted, he was brought to Richmond, Virginia, and was indicted for treason.

The outcome seemed certain, but then, in yet another twist, the judge presiding at the trial surprised everyone. Chief Justice John Marshall, wishing to uphold strict legal principles, was not as eager as were many to find Burr guilty. In fact, Marshall's careful instructions called for the testimony of two witnesses regarding treasonous acts. The prosecution could not comply, and Burr was acquitted on September 1, 1807. But in spite of this reprieve, Aaron Burr's fortunes never improved. Ruined in public life and dunned by creditors, the man who had been a vote from the presidency slipped into ignominious obscurity.

Burr's adventures, schemes, and treason trial did claim national attention and the interest of the public for a while. But the headlines were soon being filled by events in Europe and by news of another individual whose actions were affecting entire nations.

If one man could be called the dominant individual outside the United States during the first half of the nineteenth century, he would most likely be Napoleon Bonaparte. Born on the island of Corsica in 1769, he was a boy when many of America's leaders were drawing so much attention to the colonies. However, it was the spirit of revolution and its spread to Europe that directly affected the young Corsican's life.

Napoleon had joined the French army and was beginning to rise by merit through its ranks even as the Terror was destroying France's social fiber. While Napoleon was achieving his first successes abroad, the French people were crying out for an end to the mindless bloodshed at home. Napoleon was a natural hero, and the people turned to him as a central figure to restore order and stability. Within a generation, the French had toppled a monarch only to welcome a man who soon made himself emperor.

Even a cursory summary of Napoleon's life and his effect upon France and the world is too broad in its scope to include in this book. However, facts about his ciphers and communication methods are of interest here. Let us consider the latter first since he was more foresighted about mechanical devices than he was about secrecy.

In the 1790s French engineer Claude Chappe had developed a message-relay system called an *aerial telegraph* by some. One of five brothers, Chappe had struggled to have his invention both noticed and funded. His chance came when the eldest brother, Ignace, won election to the legislative assembly. Ignace eventually helped Claude secure the funding needed to build a few towers or secure structures on high ground for a test between small towns. The rapidity of the message exchange impressed the assembly enough to make them open their coffers several more inches. With this monetary support, sixteen tower/stations were built from Paris to strategic Lille on the northern border with Belgium, a distance of 140 miles. In 1794 Chappe successfully exchanged messages over what was then an extraordinary distance. Even the jaded assembly members, accustomed to all manner of bizzare money requests, were so impressed that they validated Chappe's efforts with the establishment of a nationwide system.

The Chappe telegraph was an improved version of other such systems generally called *semaphore* (Greek: *seema,* a sign + *phero,* to carry). His method consisted of a post, a crosspiece (a regulator), and wooden pieces (indicators) at either end of the crosspiece. Often standing atop its own tower, but sometimes mounted on hilltops or barns, the post supported the attached segments. The regulator and indicators were moved by a series of pulleys to create various shapes, which were viewed by means of telescopes. These are Chappe's alphabet representations:

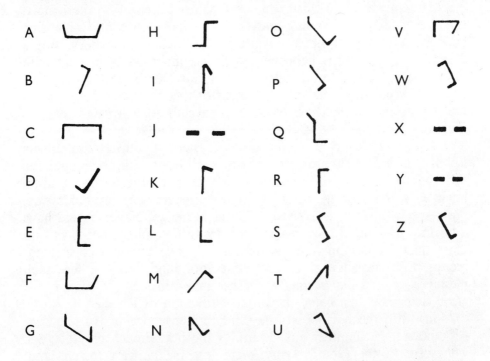

This was in essence a code but not a secret one, since the configurations were visible (on clear days) and not concealed by any transposition or substitution. The best aspect of the Chappe system was its speed. This is what most interested the "little corporal."

While Napoleon was a wise strategist and arguably the best tactician under actual battlefield conditions (pre-1860), his use of this telegraph system remained a "hidden ace" for years. Opposing generals both feared and hated him for his apparent prescience. In actuality he was able to make certain plans because he could count on the telegraph for rapid calls to secure reinforcements and supplies. Perhaps because he reaped the benefits of Chappe's creation and maintained its secret, Napoleon and historians don't credit the semaphore method with affecting the outcome of any crucial battle. However, there is evidence to indicate that one of Napoleon's strangest oversights did play a role in his eventual downfall. Great general that he was in so many respects, he did not do well with ciphers and codes.

The battle of Marengo in 1800 clearly demonstrates the links between communications and the vagaries of combat. Napoleon was engaging the Austrians near this village in the Piedmont area of northern Italy. In spite of his best planning and tactics, Napoleon's army was losing on June 14. That summer day might have changed history. But a detached French corps happened to be commanded by a man with sharp hearing. That commander, Gen. Louis Desaix de Veygoux, ordered a forced march toward the sound of specific patterns of cannon fire. His troops arrived just in time to save the day for the Corsican genius.

Napoleon never did have an elaborate system of couriers and ciphers to link his various subordinates. His own pride, his officers' prejudices, and the logical fear of interception all caused him to frown upon involved secret writing. After all, it was General de Veygoux's ears, not a special code, that averted defeat at Marengo. Napoleon did have a favorite masking device, his *petit chiffre* (little cipher), but it was no more than a common nomenclator of only two hundred or so letter groups. Still, because of his inherent command skills, a few such messages were all that seemed to be necessary through the years of his great victories. Then came the ill-fated invasion of Russia.

Along with the terrible weather and immense size of Russia, Czar Alexander I had another ally. Many of the best French cryptologists, who were in the Grand Army, were lost in the vast frozen land. Furthermore, as we learned earlier, the Russians were keenly aware of cipher secrets. The Corsican's "little cipher" would have been no match for Alexander's cryptanalysts. It is indeed fascinating to wonder to what extent these factors combined in Napoleon's most devastating reversal.

A cipher failure was a direct factor in Napoleon's second major defeat a year later in the "Battle of Nations." From October 16 to 19, 1813, near Leipzig, a town in Prussia, Napoleon was engaged with an allied force of English, Belgian, Prussian, and Austrian troops. He had hoped to make an orderly withdrawal from Leipzig and sent ciphered orders to his reserve subordinate, Marshal Augereau. The marshal was to advance to the town, hold the main Elster River bridge, and build temporary bridges. Augereau's garbled cipher reply was understood by some of Napoleon's officers to be an affirmative response. Instead, the marshal's forces not only arrived in disarray but the Elster bridge was inexplicably blown up. Trapped, Napoleon and remnants of his shattered army had to flee for their lives.

The Little Corporal's time of contemplation while in exile on Elba apparently did not include changes in his missive systems or ciphers. After escaping the island and gathering a new army, he cleverly attacked the allies where they least expected an assault—in Belgium. But two major setbacks occurred in the form of confused messages and orders.

On June 16, 1815, at the crossroads town of Quatre-Bras, French Marshals Michel Ney and Jean d'Erlon exchanged orders that were misunderstood. Instead of supporting Ney, d'Erlon's corps lost time marching between Ney's forces and Napoleon's army at Ligny. Thus, d'Erlon's corps helped neither commander, and Ney lost his advantage at Quatre-Bras. Ney had lost this opportunity while fighting an opponent named Wellington. Two days later, Wellington was defending stronger positions near a town called Waterloo.

The historic battle of Waterloo hinged on many factors beyond the scope of this text. Nevertheless, it can be said that at a very crucial point, Napoleon's army had an acute communications lapse. Napoleon had sent French Marshal Emmanuel de Grouchy in pursuit of Prussian General Gebhard von Blücher. But by 4:00 P.M. on that fateful June day, Grouchy had not yet made contact. Neither by courier nor cipher did Napoleon learn about Blücher's location until the Prussians' advance units appeared on Napoleon's right flank. As the French elite Imperial Guard was checked by Wellington and his "thin red line," Marshal Grouchy was engaging Blücher's rear guard in the town of Wavre eight miles to the east. Grouchy never entered the struggle at Waterloo, where the Corsican's last vestiges of empire were lost in the bloody Belgian fields.

11

CODES BY ANY OTHER NAME

‹‹‹

One of the best-known means of communicating information is called a code but it is actually not a secret code. Nor was it developed for use as one. In fact, the method's inventor began a professional career in the art world.

Samuel Finley Breese Morse was born in Charlestown, Massachusetts in 1791. He graduated from Yale and studied art at London's Royal Academy from 1811 to 1815. After further training with renowned artist Benjamin West, Morse returned to America with real skills and high hopes. But he found patrons scarce and had to settle for the uncertain life of an itinerant artist. For a time he even tinkered with designs for a water pump, hoping to make extra money.

In 1824 he set up more permanent lodgings in New York City. With his European training and his growing collection of sketches and oils, he found a niche for himself. The expanding, culturally aware city not only provided many art lovers but backers as well. After another year Morse's status had so improved that he was offered a valuable commission for a portrait of the Marquis de Lafayette.

This new financial security enabled Morse to broaden his artistic activities and experiment with mechanical devices, too. This hobby was secondary to his art interests while he traveled to Europe to study the works of the great masters. But during one trans-Atlantic voyage in 1832, the balance of his interests began to shift.

On a return voyage from France, a fellow passenger named Charles T. Jackson showed him a curious item. It was a crude device for sending electricity over distances. Back in New York, Morse developed his own ideas for transmitting messages across the miles.

At a laboratory on the grounds of New York University, he developed the breakthrough notion of using an electromagnet. An electric current from the sender energized an iron armature which was drawn to the magnet. This made a V-shaped alteration in the otherwise straight line being traced by a pen on paper as it moved past the armature.

From this functioning but crude message creator, Morse and his friend Alfred Vail perfected the magnetic telegraph in Morristown, New Jersey. Then Morse had his second crucial idea, the dot-dash pattern. When the sender's current of brief duration made a quick alteration in the receiver's armature, the armature's ink pen printed a dot on the moving paper. A longer-lasting current made the armature-pen attachment form a dash. In simplified terms, a sender made signals by closing and opening an electric circuit. The receiver's armature recorded the signals, and the dot-dash system provided translation into numbers and letters. Soon a telegraph key made this process more rapid.

In February 1838 Morse sent the world's first telegraph message: "Attention, the Universe, by Kingdom's Right Wheel." However, his best-remembered words were electronically transmitted six years later between Baltimore, Maryland, and Washington, D.C., when he sent the phrase, "What hath God wrought?" Soon thereafter Morse wisely founded a company of his own for the promotion of his invention, and in 1854 the United States Supreme Court fully recognized his patent. Thus, a man who had dreams of creating beautiful art in oils saw his former hobby become an important form of communication.

This chart lists Morse Code (I) and International Morse Code (II), a variation formulated in 1851 by a convention of nations that met to standardize such message systems.

	I	II
A	·—	·—
B	—···	—···
C	·· ·	—·—·
D	—··	—··

	I	II
E	·	·
F	·—·	··—·
G	——·	——·
H	····	····

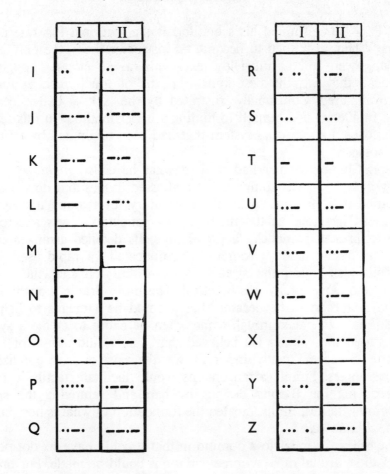

	I	II
I	..	..
J	-.-.	.---
K	-.-	-.-
L	-	.-..
M	--	--
N	-.	-.
O	..	---
P	.....	.--.
Q	..-.	--.-

	I	II
R	. ..	.-.
S	...	...
T	-	-
U	..-	..-
V	...-	...-
W	.--	.--
X	.-..	-..-
Y	.. ..	-.--
Z	.... .	--..

While not exactly in the province of secret languages or codes, major advances were made in benefiting the vision-impaired during the 1800s. The best-known of these advances—Braille—was named for the man who devised the system.

On January 4, 1809, Louis Braille was born in Coupvray, France. He was blinded by an accident with a tool at age three. Like other less fortunate people in those days, he was the object of everything from ridicule to blatant cruelty. Yet because he had the courage to persevere, he received an education with sighted children. He patiently developed the skills of a retentive mind and learned by listening to his teachers.

In Paris he continued his schooling at the National Institute of the Blind. When he trained to become an instructor there, the only books available were almost unwieldy texts with raised letters. Though impractical, this was the best known means of touch reading for the vision-impaired. Continually frustrated by the lack of better learning tools, Braille applied himself to finding a better method. In this search, he discovered an unusual system that had been originated by a French army officer.

Capt. Charles Barbier had devised what he called *night writing* or *sonography,* a system composed of embossed dashes and dots. Barbier had tried to fulfill the needs of the military for reading messages in darkness. Ingenious as the method was, sonography was affected by the ever-present battlefield factor of time. Its detailed arrangement of dots and dashes made it somewhat complicated for rapid use.

Braille also found the system awkward but felt that the general principle of sonography was practical. The more Braille thought about it, the more certain he became that it could be a means to help the blind. His own breakthrough came when he chose to create a system with raised dots alone. He believed that dots would allow for better spacing on paper. Equally important was the sense of conceptualization by the fingers. Simple arrangements would facilitate tactile learning. By reducing the Barbier designs by half and removing the space-consuming dashes, Braille created the foundation of what is now known as the *Braille cell.*

The cell was similar to a domino in that it could have six dot points. From these a total of sixty-three variations could be made. For orderly arrangement the six possible dots per cell were numbered 1, 2, 3 downward (left) and 4, 5, 6 downward (right).

Each of the twenty-six letters of the English alphabet is indicated by a differing arrangement of dots. The pattern for *a* to *j* is made from dots 1, 2, 4, and 5.

A • C • • E • G • • I • •

B • D • • F • • H • • J • •

Letters *k* to *t* are formed with the addition of dot #3 to the others. *U* to *z* are formed by using combinations of all six dots:

K • O • • S • • W • •

L • P • • T • • X • •

M • • Q • • U • • Y • •

N • • R • • V • • Z • •

Capitalization, numbers, and punctuation are just some of the variations made possible by this system. Capital letters are indicated by dot 6 being placed just to the left of a letter formation (• is capital *A*). Dots 3, 4, 5, and 6 form a kind of "reverse L" (•) to indicate that the dot groups that follow are numbers. The dots for *a* to *j* are used as the numbers 0 to 9 (• before • (B) = the number 2). Punctuation marks are indicated by dots in the lower part of the cell. The following are examples of numbers and punctuation marks:

1 • 6 • • : • •

2 • 7 • • ! • •

3 • • 8 • • . • •

4 • • 9 • ; •

5 • • 0 • •

Having considered the method, can you discern the meaning of this word?

It is *sonography,* the system that inspired Braille. When Braille's system was officially published in 1829, it included formations for music, mathematics, and science. Braille continued his work at the National Institute and made some journeys to promote his method. While he taught, he continued to make improvements. His influence on the visually impaired was direct. Using his original cells plus notations for science, math, and music, students became skilled at taking notes and even composing paragraphs. They did this with a metal rule, a stylus, a board, and paper.

The rule had open spaces. Heavy paper was placed between the rule and the board. As the rule was passed over the paper, the stylus was applied to poke through the openings and thus create the dot groupings.

This advancement, added to Braille's obvious contribution with his cells, would seem today to make him clearly worthy of acceptance. Yet France had its own series of staid traditions and entrenched, self-promoting groups. On January 6, 1852, Louis Braille passed away. Two years later his method was finally given the official approval he and it had long deserved.

During this same time, an Englishman was beginning to develop a somewhat different means of teaching the visually impaired. He was motivated by very personal reasons.

William Moon was born in Kent, England. At his birth in 1818 he was a healthy baby. However, by his fourth birthday, it was becoming increasingly obvious that he was having vision problems. Eventually, Moon was confronted with the stark certainty that he was going blind.

The miracle healing for which he no doubt must have longed did not occur. By his twenty-second year, in 1840, he had completely lost his sight. While he admired the Braille system, he believed another method was needed to help people who had lost their sight later in life. Braille was most beneficial to the young with their swifter learning capabilities. Moon correctly realized that older people, not trained in Braille from childhood, tended to have difficulties adapting to its use.

Preparing for his loss of sight, Moon had studied different training styles. He knew them well and indeed earned a living teaching blind children. But because he was aware of the learning difficulties of the middle-aged and elderly, he devoted himself to developing another kind of raised sign or figure. By the 1840s Braille was well established, and there were no practical ways to alter its sound framework. Thus, Moon sought an alternative embossed-type system.

He found his answer in a style based on Roman capital letters, some of which he varied so that they would be more clearly discernible. Suppose a student of this system tactually "read" this pattern:

L ⊔ N ∧ \   ‒ ⅃ ⌐ ⌐

If he had done his homework, the student would know that the pattern spelled *Lunar type,* a name often associated with Moon's creation and his name. By the 1880s the Lunar/Moon type had been standardized as follows:

A	∧	H	⊙	O	O	V	V
B	↳	I	∣	P	⌐	W	⌒
C	C	J	⌡	Q	⌐	X	>
D	⊃	K	<	R	\	Y	⅃
E	⌐	L	∟	S	/	Z	Z
F	⌐	M	⌐	T	‒		
G	∩	N	N	U	⊔		

Unlike Braille, Moon did live to see his efforts receive official recognition and acceptance on different educational levels. Still, Braille, Moon and Morse had much in common. Their inventiveness and personal courage gave others a chance to have the world "at their fingertips."

CRYPTANALYST'S CHAMBER III

QUIZ 1

The Culper-Tallmadge alphabet is needed to solve this double-coat (double-agent) dilemma. Prepare your own alphabet chart using the Culper-Tallmadge example and place equated numbers above and below the line (e.g., a = 1; e = 5) to discover the names of these famous patriots. (Answers on page 257.)

1. 27 30 40   48 6 40 10 12 30 8 42 32 30

2. 10   26 30 32 50

3. 30 14 46 14 30 14

4. 40   6 12 6 27 40

5. 46 32 30   40 42 14 44 8 14 30

6. 25   12 6 30 30 6 8 10

7. 16 30 6 30 26 25 12 30

8. 30 32 10 10 6 27 8 14 6 44

9. 30   10 6 25 14

10. 27   34 12 42 10 10 14 30

QUIZ 2

The Culper-Tallmadge alphabet will help you discern these terms and tools of Colonial spies. Once you've determined how the numbers were created, the words should become as plain as cleartext. (Answers on page 257.)

1.   399 45 21 216 45 440   27 224 165

2.   32 5 7 7 45 216

3.   440 216 5 288   32 255 255 216

4.   156 5 182 288   399 27 7 224

5.   7 255   12 45 440 575 45 45 224

6.   288 255 27 399 255 224

7.   16 27 32 32 45 224   288 255 21 165 45 440

8.   156 255 224 7   7 156 5 399 399

9.   575 5 624   399 45 5 156

10.   16 255 156 156 255 575   12 483 156 156 45 440

QUIZ 3

Focus your long glass on these banners and identify ten vessels famous for exploration or military glory. (Answers on page 257.)

KEY: ☐ white; ■ black; ▦ red; ▦ blue; ▦ yellow.

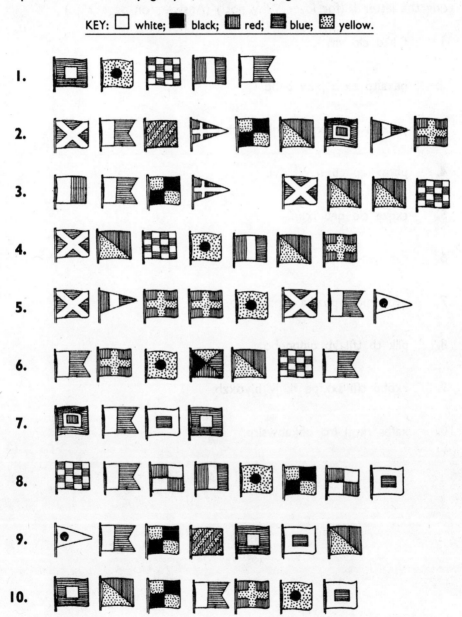

QUIZ 4

For better or worse, paramours have and will risk all to be together. Apply Marie Antoinette and Axel Fersen's key method and make a full alphabet using the letter L (for *love?* Why not?) (Answers on page 258.)

1. f ilkd clo vlr.

2. pexaltp exsb jxkv bvbp.

3. ybtxob qeb bxpq dxqbhbbmbo.

4. pbosxkqp ebxo qll tbii.

5. txqze clo qeb ixjm.

6. rpb qeb cfopq zloofalo.

7. qebk qxhb pbzlka pqxfozxpb.

8. pllk tb tfii yb qldbqebo.

9. zxobp tfii sxkfpe fk jv bjyoxzb.

10. xafbr rkqfi lro obkabwslrp.

QUIZ 5

Take a turn with Thomas Jefferson's cipher wheel. There is an extra twist here, because you need to know two key names: (a) his Virginia home and (b) the first word of his famous land deal. From the former take the first (1), third (3), and tenth (10) letters and find them on the wheel to determine the left-hand column below. From key name (b), use the fourth (4) and ninth (9) letters for the right-hand column. Then, with the wheel letter rows aligned with these keys, find the standard alphabet/number equivalents and begin. (Answers on page 258.)

1.   (3) G × (4) K = _____

2.   (1) Q − (9) D = _____

3.   (10) E + (4) U = _____

4.   (1) T ÷ (9) D = _____

5.   (10) X × (4) G = _____

6.   (3) U − (4) C = _____

7.   (10) Q × (9) P = _____

8.   (1) W + (9) Y = _____

9.   (3) R ÷ (4) C = _____

10.   (1) V × (9) U = _____

QUIZ 6

Refer to the Chappe signal method to identify these people, places, and events that affected the life of Napoleon Bonaparte. (Answers on page 258.)

1. ⌐ ∟ ∫ ⌐ ⌐ ⌐ ⌣

2. ⌐ ⌣ ⌐ ⌣ ⌄ ⌐ ⌐ ⌣

3. ⌐ ⌣ ∫ ⌐ ⌣ ⌐

4. ∟ ⌐ ⌐ ⌐ ⌐ ⌐ ⌣

5. ⌐ ∟ ⌐ ⌣

6. ⌣ ∟ ✓ ⌣ ⌐ ⌣ ⌐ ✓

7. ⌐ ⌐ ∟ ⌣ ⌐ ⌐ ⌐

8. ⌐ ⌐ ∟ ⌐ ⌐ ⌣ ⌣ ⌐ ⌣ ⌣

9. ⌐ ⌣ ⌐ ⌐ ⌐ ∟ ⌣ ⌣

10. ⌐ ⌐　⌐ ⌐ ∟ ⌐ ⌣ ⌣

QUIZ 7

Morse Code has helped save many lives during national emergencies. The American Morse version will help you uncover these newsmaking events. (Answers on page 258.)

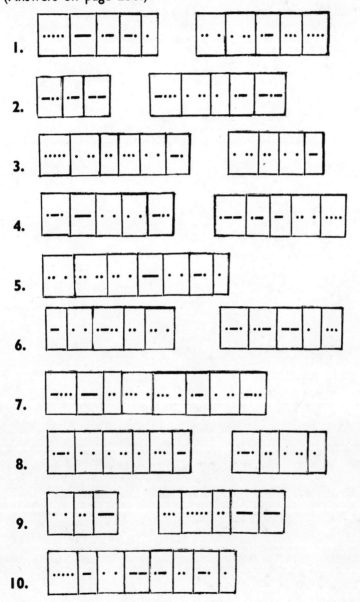

QUIZ 8

The creativity of Louis Braille was admirable. Remember his dots and cells to determine the missing numbers *between* those represented here by the Braille dots. Then find the answers according to the directions of the mathematical signs. (Answers on page 258.)

1. ⠁ -- ⠣ + ⠔ -- ⠆

2. ⠧ -- ⠐ − ⠈ -- ⠠

3. ⠦ -- ⠲ × ⠒ -- ⠢

4. ⠒ -- ⠣ + ⠒ -- ⠰

5. ⠉ -- ⠡ ÷ ⠄ -- ⠢

6. ⠛ -- ⠪ − ⠦ -- ⠂

7. ⠦ -- ⠶ × ⠒ -- ⠠

8. ⠂ -- ⠡ ÷ ⠄ -- ⠉

9. ⠦ -- ⠪ − ⠒ -- ⠰

10. ⠈ -- ⠢ × ⠶ -- ⠄

QUIZ 9

William Moon's name reminds one of the planets and stars. Use the Moon method to view these constellations. (Answers on page 258.)

1. ∧ N − ∧ \ Γ /

2. C ∧ \ I N ∧

3. Ɔ \ ∧ C O

4. ⊙ J Ɔ \ ⊔ /

5. L J \ ∧

6. O \ I O N

7. ⊂ Γ \ / Γ ⊔ /

8. / Γ \ ⊂ Γ N /

9. ▬ ⊔ C ∧ N ∧

10. V Γ ꝺ ∧

QUIZ 10

The Moon system continues to be a guide as we learn more about the universe. (Answers on page 258.)

1. ˥ | L < ˥ ˩   ⌒ ∧ ˩

2. O \ ∪ | —

3. L | ˥ ⊙ —   ˩ ˥ ∨ \

4. ˥ ∧ L ∧ > ˩

5. ˥ ˥ — ˥ O \ /

6. ∧ > | /

7. C O ˥ ˥ —

8. ˥ \ ∧ V | — ˩

9. ∧ / — ˥ \ O | ⊃ /

10. N O \ — ⊙   / — ∧ \

IV.

BALAKLAVA, BULL RUN, AND BEYOND

12

CRIMEAN NONCIPHER

‹‹‹‹

The years of Queen Victoria's reign—1837 to 1901—were noted for a combination of repression in private life amidst ostentatious displays of wealth and industrial expansion. While proper servants cut white and dark meat, European colonialists sought to carve up the mineral riches of Africa and Asia. In this time of multilayered morality, cryptology came into play in several ways. It was used by star-crossed lovers and ignored by short-sighted generals.

One of the more unusual accounts of cipher developments in this period involves a scientist-inventor and what could be described as a confusion of credits. His name graces a device developed by another while his own most successful cipher bears the name of an English baron.

The creative man was Charles Wheatstone. Born in Gloucester, England, in 1802, Wheatstone had an active mind. In London he became a businessman making and selling musical instruments. His interest in different tonal qualities led to experimentation within the field of sound. These efforts helped him garner an appointment to King's College in London as professor of experimental philosophy.

In this position Wheatstone had access to materials that enabled him to study light speeds as well as principles of electricity. In 1837 he and fellow inventor William Cooke secured the first magnetic telegraph patent. But they failed to develop a practical use for their creation, and their work was superseded by that of Samuel Morse. Undaunted, Wheatstone continued to study and conduct experiments in such diverse areas as vision, magnetoelectric machines, ciphers, phonetics, and underwater telegraphy. He is credited with inventing the concertina, the stereoscope, and the rheostat.

Ironically, he did not create his namesake invention, the *Wheatstone bridge.* This instrument for measuring electrical resistances was the 1833 brain child of Samuel Hunter Christie. Wheatstone became associated with Christie's device when he directed publicity toward it in 1843. The name *Wheatstone* was much better established than that of *Christie,* and when the former began testing the bridge with its battery and circuits, the results were often reported to be his, not Christie's. By a strange twist of fate, a very similar situation befell the most important contribution Wheatstone made to cryptology.

He created what he called a *rectangular cipher* for use in telegraphy. Though basically a substitution system, it was actually the first digraphic cipher. His method was original because it enciphered two letters, both of which directly affected the final result. With this system, and a keyword transposition, Wheatstone was able to produce a well-shuffled alphabet. Yet in spite of these factors, his cipher bears the name *Playfair.* Before considering the cipher's structure, let us see how this happened.

Lyon Playfair was the first baron of St. Andrews. A political figure of notable influence, postmaster general, and deputy speaker of the House of Commons, Playfair also considered himself a scientist. Though his own creations merit no special mention, his influence on England's social elite was considerable.

Playfair and Wheatstone lived near each other across a London bridge. They became good friends and often entertained themselves by breaking the secret messages in the personal columns of newspapers. These sections of the papers were nicknamed "agony columns." The decipherers found the efforts of the often lonely and sometimes illicit lovers quite easy to break. Accounts of the cipher solvers' friendship indicate that it was Wheatstone who contributed the majority of the answers, though it was Playfair who actually perpetuated his own name by trying to help his friend.

At a formal dinner in 1854, Playfair introduced Wheatstone's newest cipher device to a number of dignitaries. In attendance were Home Secretary Lord Palmerston and Queen Victoria's husband, Prince Albert. These powerful men and their friends were impressed and told others. However, among their circle, Playfair's name was better known than that of Wheatstone.

Soon a few far-sighted military officials had begun to consider the method as a new system for field operations. Having first heard it called *Playfair* by their superiors, these commanders perpetuated the misnomer.

Actually, Wheatstone's creation was very practical for combat use. It required no charts, lists, or mechanical tools. Its special digraphic feature made cryptanalysis difficult. A key word transposition was used to set the cipher up. This word was easy to recall and could be changed quickly if discovered.

The cipher consisted of a group of letters placed in a square or a rectangle with twenty-five spaces for the alphabet (i and j were considered to be one letter). The key word, containing no repeating letters, was written horizontally from left to right. The remaining spaces were filled by all the unused alphabet letters. The mixed alphabet was achieved by aligning the letters in the vertical columns.

As an example, recall that Wheatstone and Playfair liked to decipher the "agony columns." With that in mind, use heart as the key word and proceed as follows:

H	E	A	R	T

The next step is to place the *unused* letters of the alphabet in their proper sequence in the remaining squares. Remember that i and j share one space:

H	E	A	R	T
B	C	D	F	G
I J	K	L	M	N
O	P	Q	S	U
V	W	X	Y	Z

To begin enciphering, divide the words chosen for the plaintext message into pairs of letters (digraphs). If double letters occur in one of these pairs, use an x to separate them. For example, the plaintext word *callers* would be written as: ca lx le rs. Also use an x to make pairs in words containing odd numbers of letters. For example, the plaintext *reply* would be: re pl yx.

A given message can be enciphered according to a set pattern every time. Each pair of letters has a relationship both to the square and to one another. The following rules apply to the application of the Wheatstone/Playfair method.

1. The pair can appear in the same column, can be found in the same row, or can be in neither the same row nor column.

2. Letters that can be placed in the same row are enciphered by the letters on their right-hand side (e.g., h = e).

3. The rows are cyclical. Thus, the letter to the right of the final one in a row is the first (leftmost) letter in that row (e.g., g is enciphered as b).

4. Letters appearing in the same column have their equivalents in the square cell beneath them (e.g., a = d). The cyclical rule is maintained (e.g., x = a).

5. When the letters are in neither the same column nor the same row, each is exchanged for the letter found in its own row but in the column where the other letter stands. The encipherer finds the first message letter in the square. Then he moves across the row in which it is located until he meets the column where the second plaintext letter lies. The letter of the square at the intersection of column and row becomes the first cipher letter. To find the second cipher letter, the encipherer finds the second message letter. He moves across the row from it until intersecting the column where the first plaintext letter lies.

Naturally, these rules seem quite confusing when described in the abstract. So let's apply them to an actual message that might have appeared in a newspaper's personal column. Suppose the message is lovers leave at dawn. Placed in digraphs, the result is *lo ve rs le av ex at da wn.*

To encipher the message, find the letter pair lo on the square. These two letters aren't in the same column or row. Thus, according to rule 5, find l and move across its row to the column containing o. At that intersection we find the combined ij. For simplicity, we'll choose i to be the first cipher letter. Next find o and trace to the intersection of the column where l is located. The letter at this intersection is q. Thus, iq becomes our first enciphered pair. This aspect of the method is known as *diagonal diagramming*.

Repeating this for the next pair, ve, reveals the letters w and h at the intersecting points. To encipher the next pair, rs, refer to rule 4, letters standing in the same column have their corresponding letters in the square cell under them. Therefore, rs is enciphered as fy.

The pairs le, av, and ex are enciphered according to rule 5 and the diagonal/intersection rule. The ciphered result is le = ka, av = hx, and ex = aw2.

The pair at involves rules 2 and 3. Because a and t are in the same row, a becomes the letter beside it, or r. For t, remember that the rows are cyclical, so the letter to the "right" of t is h. Hence, at becomes rh.

For the next pair, da, refer to rule 4, the column rule: l is beneath d, and d is beneath a, so the message-text letters da become enciphered ld.

Pair wn calls for rule 5: wn = zk. Our enciphered newspaper message reads:

iq wh fy ka hx aw rh ld zk

For the sake of the couple departing at sunrise, let us hope that they have a strong ladder and can make a fast getaway before decoders like Wheatstone and Playfair have found them out.

But you may be wondering, how in the world can the secret lovers be sure that the cipher is understood? First, let's assume that only they know and have exchanged the key word, heart. The person receiving this message places the word in his or her square and follows the same pattern with the remaining alphabet letters in sequence. Then the recipient deciphers the letters by reversing the aforementioned process and rules.

Looking at the square again, we see that the first two letters, iq, are on a diagonal with each other. Using the diagonal rule, the recipient decipherer finds l and o. The same is true for wh and ve, which are on diagonals. The column rule applies to fy. Instead of moving downward, the decoder moves to the letter *above* each, or r and s. A similar change occurs when reversing rule 2. Instead of using the letter to the *right,* the decipherer uses the letter to the *left.* For example, to encipher at we used rh. But to recover the original word, we cannot go to the right-hand letter again. We must look to the left. To recover t, the cyclical effect directs us to look to the left of h. Since there is no cell there, we go to the end of the row to find t.

If Wheatstone and Playfair had had their way, the Wheatstone cipher might have become an integral part of British diplomatic and military planning. However, the attention of much of Great Britain's political and foreign service hierarchy was being drawn away from considering both the new and the (supposedly) experimental. Instead, international circumstances were causing England's leaders to depend on familiar, trusted tactics and methods. Very real problems were developing with the unpredictable Czar of Russia. This conflict came to be known as the Crimean War.

Crimea was a peninsula of Russia on the northern shore of the Black Sea. This area became the focal point of battle amidst a series of disputes regarding territorial claims and religious interests between Russia, Turkey, and provincial regions around the Black Sea.

One central factor in these disputes was distrust of Russia by Turkey and her European allies. Czar Nicholas I had called Turkey (part of the Ottoman Empire) "the Sick Man of Europe." The once united Ottoman holdings were beginning to separate for various reasons. Russia began to acquire some of this territory near her own borders. In addition, Czar Nicholas was claiming to represent and protect the nearly twelve million Orthodox subjects within the Moslem-dominated regions. The Turkish leadership resented this and did not want to be a steppingstone for Russia to achieve her long-sought goals of access to more warm-water ports.

France entered the fray primarily because of the influence of Napoleon III. His throne was built upon the unsteady rubble of the Second Republic. Wishing to direct his subjects' interests elsewhere, he was glad to embroil his nation in foreign affairs. Even though this involved a patchwork alliance with centuries-old rival England, Napoleon eagerly sought this involvement.

Great Britain had no direct concerns in the Black Sea area. Yet because of her crucial involvement with India, Britain's leaders were wary of shifts in the balance of power in western Asia. Turkish possessions formed a barrier to potential Russian advances in the region. Therefore, it was at least indirectly beneficial to England to maintain the status quo.

Though there had been Russo-Turkish fighting before, the inclusion of the European powers changed the entire situation. By early 1853 the alliance against Russia included Turkey, England, France, and Sardinia (an island kingdom near Italy). Some diplomats admirably tried to settle matters peacefully, but rigid, uninformed opinion among the allies' varied publics made negotiations difficult.

By July Russia occupied the Turkish principalities of Walachia and Moldavia. France and Britain ordered their fleets to the strategic Dardanelles entrance to the Black Sea. The Czar did not answer an October ultimatum to leave the principalities. This led to intermittent land fighting. In November the Russians defeated the Turkish fleet at Sinope, Turkey. Rumors of a slaughter at Sinope resulted in a feverish clamor for action in England and France. March 28, 1854, saw both nations declare war on Russia.

The allied strategists chose to launch a major offensive in the pivotal Black Sea area. This seemed practical because of England's naval power. By attacking the Crimean port fortress of Sevastopol, the allies hoped not only to disrupt Russia's sea lanes but also to bring the fighting to the Czar's own soil.

Within months, thoughts of glory-laden, quick victories became mired like supply wagons in the mud. Soon provisions of every type became all too scarce. Though England's navy controlled the waterways, the land war became a costly stalemate. Almost inconceivably, the military leaders had failed to heed the lessons of Napoleon's disastrous invasion of Russia just forty-two years earlier. Once more the terrain and the increasingly colder weather affected and prolonged the struggle.

Telegraphy began to play a key role, but not in tactics. Rather, the telegraph enabled the press to cover this war more extensively than had ever been possible before. Thus, the news of losses due to battle, disease, and bitter cold reached Paris, London, and Moscow with shocking regularity. The increasing casualty totals had a chilling effect on the once boisterous war fever.

Ironically, neither this method of rapid communication nor the clever Wheatstone/Playfair cipher were helpful to the allied effort. It is valid to say that telegraphy could not be set up in enough locations to be practical. Yet it is tempting to wonder about all the missed opportunities to affect events more quickly. The reasons for the failure to protect messages with the new cipher are not entirely clear but were doubtless a combination of the vague procedures of outdated tradition and lack of foresight.

One can only ponder how these two methods might have changed the results of battles at such places as Inkerman, Malakhov, and Balaklava. The Balaklava confrontation is especially curious in this regard for it was the scene of the brave but tragic charge of the British Light Brigade.

Entire books have been written about this valiant but suicidal confrontation. Most people have heard about this tragedy through the verses of Alfred Lord Tennyson's classic poem. Still, after years of debate and conjecture, a mystery of confused orders and ill-conceived tactics remains.

On October 25, 1854, Russian general Prince Menshikov attacked the English base at Balaklava. Several important artillery batteries were taken, and their loss endangered the entire British position in that part of the front. A series of indecisive choices led to a fateful decision. A swift attack was needed to regain the cannons. The Light Brigade was chosen to accomplish the task because of their fast steeds and light armament.

The seventh Earl of Cardigan, James Brudenell, received orders to advance through a nearby valley. However, many questions have been raised regarding the intent and timing of this command. Neither other units nor adequate cannon fire were provided in support. No telegraph linkup existed to rescind the fateful order. Several historians and writers have even speculated that Cardigan's old enemy and brother-in-law, Lord Lucan, had somehow conspired against him by misinterpreting or misdirecting the orders. Because Lord Lucan led the division of which the Brigade was a part, he was castigated for not helping Lord Cardigan and the doomed cavalry.

While the struggle dragged on, there was enough blame for blunders to spread among all the commanders. After other costly sacrifices at the Redan and the Chernaya River, the allies finally captured Sevastopol in September 1855. By the Treaty of Paris, Russia was forced to accept a neutral Black Sea and agreed not to interfere with Turkey's internal affairs.

Of course it is pure speculation to wonder about what might have happened if orders could have been rapidly conveyed and capably enciphered. But such combinations of methods were not yet fully appreciated. Instead, many brave men marched or rode into places like Balaklava's North Valley, never to return.

13

BLUE AND GRAY

〈〈〈〈

Five years after the Crimean War ciphers and communication systems affected the outcome of the American Civil War. The Civil War (1861–65) was the first major confrontation in which the telegraph's potential was fully realized, especially by the industrially advanced Union forces. Yet it was the Confederacy that first benefited from the wise application of another signal system known as *wigwag.*

Wigwag, or *flag telegraphy,* is a system of positioning a flag (or flags) at various angles that indicate the corresponding twenty-six letters of the alphabet. This method was created in the mid-1800s by three men working in separate locations: Navy Captain Philip Colomb and Army Captain Francis Bolton, in England, and inventor-surgeon Albert J. Myer in America.

Myer had studied signaling methods during his youth and had a well-rounded knowledge of the field. While pursuing his medical studies in the summer of 1850, he worked to finance his education. His natural inclinations directed him toward a rail telegraph office in northern New York. The railroad used an electrochemical telegraph that had been developed by Alexander Bain, a Scottish scientist. This telegraph had a type of needle that moved back and forth in response to the messages it received. Some historians have suggested that this telegraph inspired Myer to develop both a touch method of communication for the deaf and later the wigwag system.

Whatever the source of Myer's inventions, he was indeed very involved in helping both the deaf and the blind. He derived a kind of manual alphabet from the Bain telegraph's alphabet that enabled one to communicate with the deaf by finger taps on a person's hand. He translated the telegraph's intervals of dashes and dots into longer or shorter taps and pauses. It seems likely that Myer was aware of the quadrilateral alphabet and prisoners' signals from his studies. Whether or not this was the case, he put his ideas together in his doctoral thesis, "A New Sign Language for Deaf Mutes."

While advancing in his career as an army surgeon, Myer perfected his wigwag flag system and companion methods with torches and disks. Myer termed his banner method, which he developed around 1856, *flag telegraphy.* Some accounts, including that of *Traditions of the Signal Corps* (1959), credit an unnamed Civil War general with the name *wigwag.* First used as a nickname for the signals' movements, the term eventually supplanted Myer's own choice.

The equipment involved appealed to the military because of its simplicity and hardiness. It could be carried easily on foot or horseback and was not too likely to be damaged by enemy fire. Standard-issue field glasses or telescopes could be used for long-distance viewing.

Three main color combinations were used in flags measuring two, four, or six feet square. The white banners had red-squared centers while the black or red flags had a center block of white. These colors were well suited for contrast with varied backgrounds (sky, hills, forests, boulders, etc.). The flagstaff itself was usually made of a strong wood such as hickory and was built in sections that could be joined for extension if needed. The method, as outlined in Myer's *Manual of Signals* (1879) required three elements (motions) to be used for each letter:

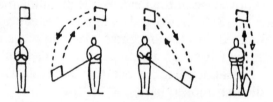

As Myer described it, the first position always initiated a message sequence. The banner was held vertically above the flagman's head. The first motion ("one," "1") was made by waving the banner toward the ground to the flagman's right, then quickly returning it to the first position. The second motion ("two," "2") was made by waving the flag toward the ground on the man's left, then returning it to the first position. The third movement ("three," "3") called for lowering the banner to the front, then restoring it to the vertical angle.

The following chart indicates how an alphabet and directional orders could be conveyed. The numbers next to each letter indicate the three positions needed to send that letter. For example, *"a"* (112) would be "waved" as motion 1, motion 1, motion 2 in rapid succession to complete the letter without a pause.

A—112	H—312	O—223	V—222
B—121	I—213	P—313	W—311
C—211	J—232	Q—131	X—321
D—212	K—323	R—331	Y—111
E—221	L—231	S—332	Z—113
F—122	M—132	T—133	
G—123	N—322	U—233	

MYER'S SIGNAL DIRECTIONS

3—*End of a word*

33—*End of a sentence*

333—*End of a message*

22.22.22.3—*Signal of assent: "I understand," or "Message is received and understood," or "I see your signals," or general affirmative*

22.22.22.333—*Cease signaling*

121.121.121.3—*Repeat*

212121.3—*Error*

211.211.211.3—*Move a little to the right*

221.221.221.3—*Move a little to the left*

As the Civil War wore on, Myer increased the wigwag motions to four. This enabled more specialized words and abbreviations to be used.

Myer also developed a similar daytime system in 1864 using standardized disks. The disks, which measured twelve to eighteen inches in diameter, generally had wood or metal frames with canvas stretched across them. The disks had handles and were held in a pattern of first position, followed by the series of motions shown here:

For night signals, Myer applied the wigwag pattern to torches and lanterns. The torches were of two varieties. The free-moving, or (*flying torch*) was attached to the staff. The *foot* torch was placed on the ground as a set point of reference. Thus, the direction of the flying torch's "wave" was better seen. The torches were metal canisters filled with oil or a similar fluid:

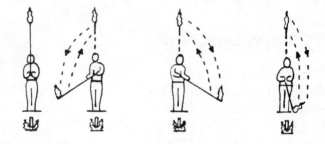

Lanterns were of a standard variety. One lantern was mounted on a pole in a fixed position. A second lantern was moved above and to either side of it.

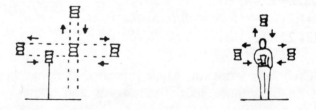

Myer prepared a report on his experiments, particularly the wigwag system, for his superiors in 1856. Though mildly complimentary, the ranking officers did not rush to incorporate his creations. Pressing onward, Myer continued testing and improving the system and its variations through 1859. One of his chief assistants was Alexander E. Porter, friend, soldier, and student of signals. Though both men were employed by the United States Army, the Civil War was soon to separate them. When it began, Porter joined the Confederate army and it was he, not Myer, who first used wigwag in actual combat. In fact, he affected the events of a battle.

On Sunday, July 21, 1861, Porter, then a captain in the Confederate army, was serving on one of four observation towers that he and Gen. P.T. Beauregard had set up and had equipped with signal flags. These towers overlooked the countryside around a Virginia rail depot called Manassas Junction. Fresh water was provided by a nearby creek, Bull Run.

During the previous night, divisions of Brig. Gen. Irvin McDowell's Union army had been moving to flank the Confederate left. After delays caused by the terrain, advance units of this force had reached Sudley Ford by 8:45 A.M. on July 21. On the verge of surprising the southern troops at an important crossing—the Stone Bridge—the Union army did not notice the sun glinting on one of their fieldpieces.

This reflection and the gleam from bayonets drew Porter's looking glass toward the ford. Danger was clearly imminent. Now all of the training he had had with Myer and his own southern loyalty made him act swiftly and skillfully. Porter sent the following flag warning to Confederate Colonel Nathan Evans at the Stone Bridge defenses: "Look out for your left, you are turned."

Colonel Evans ordered cannon and musket fire toward the Federal troops before they could initiate their attack. Porter no doubt watched with deep satisfaction as the Union troops were halted. At that moment none of the participants in this conflict could know what the successful warning would mean. However, analysts would later say that Porter's vigilance led to changes in the tactics of the entire struggle around Manassas Junction. The application of this new signal system had directly influenced the shocking Union defeat that eventful July day.

Amidst the confusion and accusations of blame following the Bull Run debacle, Myer continued his long struggle for better military communications. His fortunes and the cause of signal systems took a turn for the better on July 26, 1861. On that date Irvin McDowell was replaced by Maj. Gen. George McClellan. Myer presented his proposals to the general, who was himself seeking answers to the Union's failures. It did not take Myer long to convince him that better message-sending methods were needed. The general had known about some of the uses of telegraphy in the Crimea. He found in Myer an American of mutual ideas, but both the Congress and the powerful Secretary of War, Edwin Stanton, proved to be formidable barriers to achieving improvements. It took more actual battlefield evidence to convince them that changes were needed.

McClellan was beset by military problems through the summer of 1862. His efforts to capture Richmond, known as the Peninsula Campaign, became a series of stalemates, then costly reversals. Ironically, as his tactics began to fall into disfavor, Myer's luck in persuading some commanders to use more battlefront communications began to improve.

His case benefited from events on the Potomac River. In September 1862 General Lee initiated his first invasion of the North. Lee ordered his troops to cross the river at a remote site about thirty miles north of Washington, D.C. Lee's army was near the town of Frederick, Maryland, and advancing unchecked when one of its wagon supply units was spotted.

This support column was not discovered by regular Union scouts. Rather, it was sighted by one Lieutenant Miner, a flag signalman stationed at a post on Sugar Loaf Mountain. On September 6 the lieutenant flagged this news to the Signal Corps' base at Point of Rocks. From there, telegraph lines that ran along the Baltimore and Ohio Railroad track conveyed the alert to Washington. The Army of the Potomac was hastily ordered to march and counterattack. As events unfolded, the Union suffered more setbacks. However, General Lee's attempt to do irreparable damage was thwarted by the eagle-eyed flag officer.

These losses finally jarred the Congress and the War Department into allocating much-needed funds, which were used to purchase everything from copper wire for telegraphy to real flags for men previously training with broomsticks and tattered shirts. At long last Myer's expertise was beginning to be respected. The benefits were to be realized almost a full year after Lieutenant Miner's warning, when, at a town in southern Pennsylvania, sightings of epic proportions occurred.

General Lee had invaded northern soil again in June of 1863. On

June 24 a much better organized flag system relayed word of Lee's newest Potomac crossing. This message rapidly went from the observation post at Maryland Heights to the War Department, in spite of cut telegraph lines.

Still, the Union's high command was in disarray. On June 28 Gen. Joseph Hooker resigned, and George Meade was made commander of the Army of the Potomac. While General Meade tried to form his own chain of command, he set up temporary headquarters at Taney-town, Maryland. In the midst of calling in scattered army units, startling news came to Taneytown via signalmen on July 1. A patrol of Union General Buford's command had skirmished with Confederates at a site near the Maryland border. Soon both sides were committing larger numbers of troops to the fray. The wigwag messages made the situation clear: a major force was facing Buford and not in Maryland, but in Pennsylvania. Lee himself was in command at the town of Gettysburg.

Signalmen of each army sent out calls for help. Reinforcements rushed forward from locations dozens of miles away. By July 1, seventy-three thousand gray and eighty-eight thousand blue met in one of history's most decisive battles.

Rarely, if at all, do textbooks even hint that the secret message system of flags affected these history-changing events. Yet crucial sightings made by Union observers directly tipped the scales against Lee's best tactics.

On July 2 Union signalmen, positioned on the twin rocks called the Round Tops, discovered rebel troops in the woods near the strategic Emmitsburg Road. Reinforcements were rushed to the North's defenses there, and they thwarted a flanking attack that could have won the day for the South.

July 3 found Lee desperately trying to gain victory by planning to attack the Union's center positions. Artillery and rifle fire were extremely intense. The Round Top observers could not use their flags lest they expose themselves to sharpshooters. Nevertheless, these brave watchers continued to relay missives by courier. One such rider brought vital news to the Union's battered signal command post.

On Cemetery Ridge, Capt. David Castle received a rider's word that rebel Gen. George Pickett was beginning a massive charge against the middle of the "thin blue line." Confederate artillery barrages along the ridge had sent other flagmen rushing for cover, yet Captain Castle used a wooden pole and a bedsheet for a makeshift flag to alert Union headquarters. The message arrived in time for General Meade to act and order counter measures.

Pickett's charge was stopped short of breaching the Union lines. General Lee's desperate gamble had failed. Previously disregarded flagmen enabled George Meade to enter the shrine of heroes.

14

CIVIL WAR SPIES

<<<<

The American Civil War had a second major front in the shadowy lives of spies and their secret codes.

Though neither side maintained training centers for special agents, both benefited from such activities. As the South had first achieved success with flag signals, so did the rebels' cause prosper early because of ambitious spies.

One such agent, a Washington widow, gave the Union trouble from the outset. This clever southern Loyalist was Rose Greenhow. In her mid-forties, she was the charming widow of a prominent Washington, D.C., physician. Her reasons for siding with the Secessionists are no longer known, but her motivations must have been strong, for she conducted herself like a professional.

Greenhow used her position in the elite circles of Washington society to gain information. While men and women gathered for a respite from the war, she kept her senses keen. Her eyes noted officers' faces, and her ears picked up the slightest slip of a loose tongue. She was adept at ingratiating herself with the wives and relatives of wealthy industrialists and powerful congressmen. Greenhow's equally sharp mind held and linked rumors, gossip, and carelessly revealed facts in a mosaic of information. After much careful checking, she sent reports to rebel commanders.

Though records are vague about the specific cipher means she used for each communication, Greenhow might have used what was known as a *route*.

Rather basic in their structure, routes became popular during such trying times when speed of creation and delivery was more expedient than total secrecy. Also, because the recipients were often military men who had to act quickly, there was little time for delays in deciphering.

The route combined word transposition, code words, a plaintext set up in columns (reading up some columns and down others), enough nulls to confuse the enemy, and a preset pattern by which to read the columns. Suppose that Greenhow had sent this message to the Confederates:

```
alert 12 is coins then first strength advance
gold east village along the divisions Caesar
been has today hand cross march to x ordered
box 4 they wide the their sun rise objective
carolina ford will estimated to.
```

Since there are actual words in this message, one is tempted to try to fit sentences together. Is there to be an advance on an east village? But who is Caesar? Is he to march to a site called "x"? Who or what is carolina and what will happen at sunrise?

Lets "map" this route. By prearrangement, she and the recipient know that alert 12 is the key phrase. Neither the word alert nor the numbers 1 and 2 are to be placed in the columns of words. However, this key phrase directly governs how the columns are to be read. For example, they might be read in order 1, 2, 3, etc. or in the reverse order: 3, 2, 1, etc. The key phrase also determines how the column is to be read: up or down.

The term alert 12 actually conveys quite a bit of information. An alert is certainly a warning. The word was also chosen because of the numerical position of its own letters in the alphabet: a is the first letter, l is the twelfth, e is fifth, r is eighteenth, and t is twentieth. This tells our recipient to read the first column. But e comes before l alphabetically. This tells the recipient to read the third column, then the second, fourth, and fifth. The predetermined numbers 1 and 2 mean "read up the first column and down the second, up the third, down the fourth, and up the fifth."

Finally, alert 12 also signals the overall size of the route. The five letters and two numbers stand for five columns made up of seven words each. The receiver then knows that the seven words after the number 2 go in the first column. Since this column is to be read from bottom to top, the words would appear thus:

(1)
gold
advance
strength
first
then
coins
is

Since the arrangement of e signifies that the third column is to be read next, the 1 and 2 factor of alert 12 says the third column is to be read upwards. Therefore, we have the configuration:

(3)
been
Caesar
divisions
the
along
village
east

Returning to the 1 and 2 pattern, their reading directions are second (down), fourth (down), fifth (up). Now we have a fully constructed route. Read naturally from left to right and along each row.

(1)	(2)	(3)	(4)	(5)
gold	has	been	ordered	to
advance	today	Caesar	box 4	estimated
strength	hand	divisions	they	will
first	cross	the	wide	ford
then	march	along	the	carolina
coins	to	village	their	objective
is	x	east	sun	rise

Why doesn't it make complete sense yet? Don't forget the code words and nulls. Mrs. Greenhow wouldn't want just anyone to know these code words: gold (McDowell), Caesar (July), box 4 (16), hand (5), wide (Long), ford (Bridge), carolina (Columbia), coins (Turnpike), village (Annandale), x (Manassas).

The words *east, sun,* and *rise* are nulls that complete the five-column, seven-word arrangement. Once we place the code words in their proper sequence, we have the following plaintext message:

```
McDowell has been ordered to advance today
July 16. Estimated strength 5 divisions. They
will first cross the Long Bridge then march
along the Columbia Turnpike to Annandale.
Their objective is Manassas.
```

"Rebel Rose" Greenhow did send a missive to the Confederate defenders of Manassas Junction. Historians credit her with providing information about Union troop movements and numbers that helped General Beauregard and his allies in arms that fateful day.

This early success was followed by a series of communications that Greenhow conveyed in everything from pockets hidden in clothing to coded designs embroidered in dresses. Eventually her achievements for the Secessionists caused Federal authorities to react. They increased their own numbers of agents and began detailed tracing of party and parlor gossip to its sources.

Washington social circles were close knit, and "Rebel Rose" had an increasingly difficult time hiding her double life. Her chief nemesis was none other than that pioneer of detectives, Allan Pinkerton. By a combination of luck and determined effort, Pinkerton was eventually able to trap, arrest, and place Greenhow in Old Capitol Prison.

Undaunted, she created new links to her old network from her prison cell. Eventually, Union officials granted her amnesty and sent her to Richmond. Praised there as a heroine, Greenhow was given a new assignment by Jefferson Davis. She gladly accepted and went to gain sympathy for the South in London and Paris.

Another Confederate woman possessing much bravery and cunning was Belle Boyd. This West Virginia native was only eighteen years old in 1861. She has often been depicted in stories and campfire songs as being an adventuresome courier riding daringly through the Shenandoah Valley. Her messages are credited with one direct military result: her report about Union troop activities near Front Royal, Virginia, enabled Gen. Stonewall Jackson to make a successful attack there.

The Federal government also had its secret agents as well as sympathizers south of the Mason-Dixon Line. One very capable woman perhaps succeeded largely because she seemed to be an unobtrusive spinster.

In her early fifties, mild-mannered Elizabeth van Lew moved quietly about Richmond, Virginia, with her heart directed northward. In addition to providing facts about Richmond's defenses, she helped Union prisoners escape from the infamous prisons of Belle Isle and Libby. While these men recuperated, van Lew hid them in her Church Hill mansion. Upstairs she compiled detailed facts that were important for General Grant's strategic plans in his siege of the Secessionists' capital.

A second Union Loyalist was Pauline Cushman. An actress of New Orleans Creole ancestry, Cushman was in her late twenties when she was asked to help the North with her theatrical abilities. While performing in Nashville in May 1863, she agreed to travel to Shelbyville, Tennessee. There she pretended to be a rebel sympathizer evicted from her former surroundings. While in Shelbyville, she gained favor with residents and military staffers. Using her acting skills of memorization, she conveyed news about Gen. Braxton Bragg and the Confederate forces based in the area. Cushman's information soon helped Union commander William Rosecrans when he victoriously captured the town.

Some of the methods used by these courageous women and others have been obscured by the years and the secrecy of their efforts. Most of the ciphers were simple homemade symbol, number, and letter combinations. However, in addition to personal letter or number codes, and an occasional Vigenère-style cipher, another form was often used during the era: the *rail fence.*

A method of transposition, the rail fence seems to have gotten its name from its fencelike appearance, which is the result of aligning rows of letters, then shifting them. For example, let us apply this method to the phrase Grant led the North.

We begin enciphering by counting the number of letters in the message. In this case the total is 16, which is a multiple of 4. As we shall soon see, this is good. If the total were odd, we would have to add nulls at the end to make a multiple of 4 such as 20, 24, or 28. Then we write the message with every other letter slightly lower, as shown:

G   A   T   E   T   E   O   T
 R   N   L   D   H   N   R   H

Next we copy the top row of letters and place the bottom row directly alongside it:

GATETEOTRNLDHNRH

Enciphering is then made more complex by using a four-letter group that makes word divisions difficult to find. The completed cipher text would be:

GATE   TEOT   RNLD   HNRH

Letter variations can be achieved by writing them with one row backward and the other forward, or by reversing both of them:

(A) Backward/Forward: GATETEOTHRNHDLNR
     Enciphered: GATE   TEOT   HRNH   DLNR

(B) Reversed: HRNHDLNRTOETETAG
     Enciphered: HRNH   DLNR   TOET   ETAG

Another variation can be created by a three-part fence in an almost zigzag pattern:

G   T   T   O
 R   N   L   D   H   N   R   H
   A   E   E   T

These letters put into cipher would be:

GTTO   RNLD   HNRH   AEET

Deciphering such messages is relatively simple. Let's begin with our first enciphered message. Use a vertical line to split the letters into two equal halves:

GATE TEOT | RNLD HNRH

Then search for the original words by listing letters in the following order: First letter on the left side of the line G, first letter on the right side R, not H, second on the left A, second on the right N, etc. Of course, the letters aren't segmented into words. However, the recipient is expected to have some knowledge of the contents' purpose and therefore could make better sense of even a null-filled sentence than could an outsider.

Regarding the reversed or backward/forward styles, the recipient would not be able to use this same vertical-line method, but he or she would be forewarned to be aware of the extra complications and would have the means to reorder the letters accordingly.

This method was popular with generals, soldiers, and spies alike because it was relatively easy to learn and apply. No doubt spies like Belle Boyd or Federal detectives led by Allan Pinkerton dealt with a number of messages in route or rail-fence form. However, historians have never pinpointed a specific code or cipher that affected the Civil War's outcome in the same way that one communication system did. That system was telegraphy, and it was the more industrialized North that used it to best advantage.

By 1864 Federal commander Ulysses S. Grant was initiating a grueling war of attrition with General Lee. Struggles in places like Spotsylvania Court House, the Wilderness, and Cold Harbor led to a mounting casualty list. But these confrontations were different from those costly battles fought previously at Gettysburg, Chancellorsville, and Antietam.

General Lee was being forced to protect his beloved Virginia soil and its capital, Richmond. No longer was Lee able to move with the quick strikes and clever flanking movements of his earlier offensives. Now he was on the defensive, hemmed in by Union numbers, firepower, and especially technology.

General Grant was combining massive factory production, miles of railroads, and a virtual forest of telegraph poles to encircle his opponent. It was telegraph keys and gleaming copper wires that outraced the fastest rebel couriers. Messages sent by Grant's telegraphy bases had Federal troops arriving at strategic points before Lee's farsighted plans could be enacted. Telegraphy and Morse Code enabled Grant to have a broad-scale strategy that was unknown in previous warfare. He could literally be commanding in one battle while he sent and received ciphered messages from other fronts. Only a similarly equipped army would have had an equal chance against these factors. But the decimated South could not provide its troops with such advantages.

15

FROM EAST TO WEST

<<<<

The painful legacy of the Civil War continued to haunt the nation long after Appomattox. In fact, some eleven years after its conclusion, both the festering ill-will and secret ciphers affected a contested presidential election.

In 1876 Samuel J. Tilden, governor of New York, was the Democratic party's nominee. He opposed Ohio's governor, Rutherford B. Hayes. Both men had a reputation for personal honesty. However, the political spoils system and its corruption had spread like a plague through the state capitals and Washington, D.C. Furthermore, a number of southern states were still being controlled by carpetbaggers and self-serving profiteers. Voting procedures and regulations nationwide had not been standardized. All of these factors led to the most bitterly disputed presidential election in American history.

According to the most reliable popular vote totals, Tilden had won by two hundred fifty thousand or so votes. However, the Electoral College remained in dispute. Conflicting returns from Oregon, South Carolina, Florida, and Louisiana had placed the final number in doubt. Because of this, Tilden and the Democrats were one electoral vote short of the presidency, with a total of one hundred eighty-four.

Congress set up an election commission made up of five members each of the Supreme Court, Congress, and the Senate. This group was anything but impartial during its investigation. For about four months claims of improper conduct and influence peddling were regularly heard or printed. When the commission finally placed each state's electoral votes in the Republicans' column, the members did so on a rigid party-line vote of eight to seven. All of the disputed twenty-two votes were given to Hayes and made his the winning total of one hundred eighty-five. Though the Democrats raised an outcry of fraud, the commission's decision stood, and Rutherford B. Hayes became our nineteenth president. Though never directly implicated in anything illegal, Hayes's otherwise productive administration was irrevocably tainted by the election dispute.

However, few accounts of this period ever mention that some of Tilden's closest associates, including his nephew, were actually exposed in a scheme to buy votes. The exposé was conducted by the *New York*

Tribune, and its basis was a series of twenty-seven enciphered telegrams.

The Western Union telegrams were secretly given to the newspaper by someone on a congressional investigating committee. The still-enciphered messages were revealed in the *Tribune* during the summer of 1878. In this tantalizing format they created quite a stir. Readers and amateur cryptanalysts began sending in attempted solutions. Eventually, a *Tribune* editor, the paper's economic writer, and a mathematician at the Washington, D.C. Naval Observatory each independently broke the ciphers.

The cipher types included: word transpositions, dictionary-based code words, and monalphabetic substitutions using pairs of numbers. Their solutions provided irrefutable evidence that William Pelton, Tilden's nephew, had bargained and offered bribes for votes. Most damning was the proof that some of Pelton's correspondence had been mailed to 15 Gramercy Square, Tilden's New York home.

Tilden told the congressional group that he was completely unaware of his nephew's actions. He testified that if any scheming had occurred, it had been done without his knowledge. But while no charges were ever brought against the Democratic candidate, his reputation was ruined. The man who had been one electoral vote from the presidency was denied a second chance by the cipher revelations.

While these political disputes held the interest of many, the attention of others was being drawn elsewhere by the "talking trees" and the "iron horses"—telegraphy and railroads, respectively. These two innovations were closing the distances between our coasts and borders ever more rapidly during the development of the West. Though this crucial period of our country's growth did not witness an application of ciphers like that of the Civil War, a new kind of two-part language was entering the nation's consciousness. This was the dual pictograph and sign language of the first Americans, the Indians.

Prior to 1865 only a relatively small number of frontier-dwelling trappers, explorers, and settlers had been familiar with the many and diverse Indian tribes. But with the tens of thousands of former city residents, immigrants, and displaced battle veterans seeking a different life beyond the Mississippi, new chapters of national history began to unfold. Through both peaceful relations and tragic conflicts, the native Americans' methods of communicating no longer remained a secret.

Many of the Indians recorded their long and honored past by means of pictographs, picture writings/drawings that represent ideas. They also exchanged facts by means of sign language. Let us first consider the former, an art form used for communication.

Like hieroglyphics, pictographs have a long and involved history that developed over many centuries. A number of Indian tribes employed drawings that were distinctive both to their tribe and geographic region. For many years, these differences made the gathering of common symbols for even two Indian tribes very difficult. Today, however, thanks to author William Tomkins, we have a much better understanding of these drawings. In his fine book, *Indian Sign Language,* Tomkins gives many examples of the pictographs used by the North American Sioux and Ojibwa Tribes. The descriptions and samples presented are largely based on his research compiled while he lived near the Sioux Reservation in the Dakota Territory. He, in turn, had secured facts from Indian cultural studies made in the 1800s by men such as Lt. Col. Garrick Mallery and Henry Schoolcraft, an official with the Bureau of Indian Affairs.

The Ojibwa and Sioux symbol drawings are basic representations of nature, people, animals, and objects. They are not intended to be artistically detailed but rather are drawn so as to be easily understood. For example, the sun and moon are depicted as follows:

Sunrise and sunset are similarly depicted, with a directional mark added:

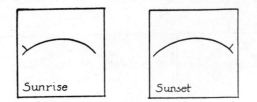

A topic as complicated as time is given more detail, as follows:

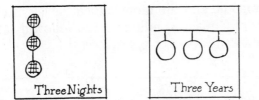

Tomkins also researched the Indians' lunar-based time system. As verified for him by the American Indian Association, the following chart indicates one year's progress in pictographs:

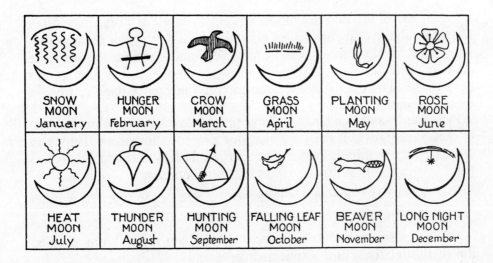

Because of their close relationship with and deep respect for every aspect of the physical world, Indians often interpret and identify natures' creatures. Some examples are:

Equally important to Indians are the whims of the weather. In the past both the nomadic and the more settled village dwellers had to be constantly aware of climatic conditions. The following are pictographic interpretations of some weather conditions:

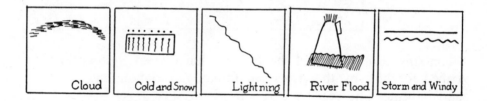

When the Sioux or the Ojibwa wished to relate a story, they often placed symbolic drawings on an animal skin. To interpret the account, one begins in the center, reads to the left, and continues around the circular route to the final symbol or figure at the end of the spiral's outer edge. This pictographic account on the facing page is from a Sioux document.

Pictography and sign language have several developmental similarities. In fact, historians still debate which one preceded the other. They also share a number of basic syntactic properties. Tomkins' research revealed the following central aspects of Indian sign language:

1. The gender of a sign is indicated by adding the signs for woman or man to it.

2. Prepositions, adverbs, adjectives, etc., are rarely given detailed use in the relatively uncomplicated sentences.

3. *A, an,* and *the* do not have their own distinct signs.

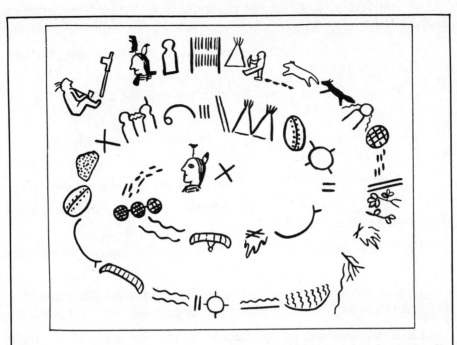

The characters in these pictographic stories are arranged in a spiral formation, the course of the spiral being from right to left, starting from right center and reading backwards. This form is used in Lone Dogs' Winter Count and certain other famous Sioux documents.

Interpretation of Above Pictographic Story

An Indian trader by the name of Little Crow went on a journey. He traveled for three nights until he came to a river. The reason he traveled at night was because he was in enemy country. At the river he secured a canoe, camped there that evening, and at sunrise the next morning started down the river and traveled two suns (days). He now traveled in daytime, because he was in friendly territory. He was an Indian trader in shells, which were used for wampum and ornamentation. At the end of the fifth day's travel he reached the village where the shells were obtainable. He rested there for three days in conference with the chief, and as a result he traded for a large amount of shells, and at sunrise on the fourth day he loaded his canoe and started down the river and traveled for two days. On the second day a storm came up, with rain and lightning. He saw the lightning strike a tree and set it afire. As a result of the storm he became sick, so he searched and found some medicinal plants and waited there a couple of days until he felt better. He then traveled at night and hid away in the day time. He knew that the country abounded in game because he heard foxes and wolves. He finally reached home, though some days late. Twenty braves of the tribe came out to meet him, including their chief, Standing Bear. Their hearts were glad as a result of his safe and successful trip, and they all had a very sociable time.

4. The first person singular pronoun, *I,* is depicted by gesturing to one's self.

5. The first person plural pronoun, *we,* is shown by using the sign for *all* and the one for *me.*

6. *You* (singular) is shown by pointing with the right hand at the person being addressed.

7. *You* (plural) is indicated by the same means as in #6, then adding the sign for *all.*

8. *They* is indicated by combining the gestures for *he* and *all.*

9. One's age is shown by the number of winters that have passed since the day of one's birth.

10. Present time is indicated by the sign for *today* and the one for *now.*

11. For the time of day, the gesture for *sun* is used while directing one's hand toward the sun's actual position at the time indicated.

12. Every question is preceded by a question sign. Thus, *when, why,* and all other *wh-* inquiries begin with the same gesture. The sentence "What are you making?" is signed as: *Question, you, make.*

Here are examples of Indian pictographs and sign language:

Woman   Soldier   Medicinal Plants   Canyon   Prayer

See   Hunt   Plenty Corn   Bird Tracks   Sioux

Spirits Above   Man   Council   Walked   Strong

Cheyenne   Talk (intense)   Road   Crane   Travois

Mandan   Eagle Tail   Ropes Horses   Man disabled   Buffalo

Medicine Man   Hear   Singing   Drum and Stick   Peace Pipe

Calling for Rain   Deep Snow   Making Peace   Wind   Cactus

Eagle   Wise Man   Ran   Direction   Boy

Girl

Call for

Black Deer

Man on horse back

Talk together

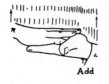

Goose

Mountain

White Man

Dear Tracks

Long Hair

Add

Camp

Bag

Fire

Island

Horse

Sit or Remain

Arise

Possession

House

See

No

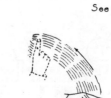

Question

I or Me

Recover

Teepee

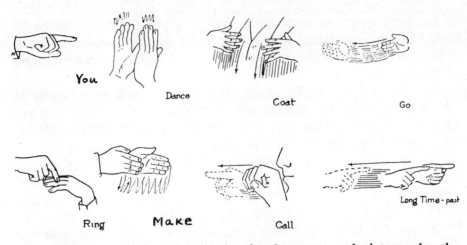

In addition to communicating by sign language and pictographs, the Plains Indians were especially adept at using smoke signals. Like the ancients, the Indians used different space and time intervals between the smoke puffs to convey messages from mesa to valley and woodland to prairie. This skill became especially vexing to the United States Army and its cavalry units, which were assigned to patrol the vast lands between the Mississippi, the Missouri, and the Rio Grande rivers. Military leaders believed that smoke signals gave Indian warriors a definite edge. Because wigwag was limited by terrain and weather and telegraph wires and poles were vulnerable targets, the army initiated a mechanism called the *heliograph* (Greek: *helios,* sun + German: *graphein,* to write).

This instrument was being used by civilians and European military forces alike during the latter part of the nineteenth century. It varied in design according to the needs of the particular region. The version used by the Plains army units had a mirror and a sighting vane similar to those in the figure shown. Some versions also had two mirrors, both of which were mounted on a tripod.

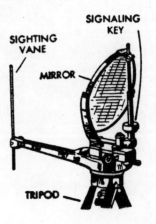

The heliograph required bright sunshine for optimum efficiency. Reflected light was altered by the use of a screen or shutter attached

to a second tripod in accordance with a Morse dot-dash pattern. A longer shutter application was a dash and a shorter one was a dot. A change in position relative to the sun required a different configuration of the mirrors.

With the sun before the sender, the light was reflected directly to the receiving station as aligned by the sighting vane. If the sender had the sun at his back, the rays were reflected with the two-mirror arrangement. From the second one, messages went to the recipient.

Weather, terrain, and mirror size all placed some limits on the heliograph, but one advantage was definitely apparent. On a good day, men with unaided eyes could see a flash from a distance of thirty miles. Visibility could be further enhanced by using field glasses or telescopes. By such a rapid traversing of distance, the heliograph was able to supplant the telegraph in remote locales for several years.

In closing it should be noted that more than a few clever Indians interrupted and confused these optical signals with their own mirrors. Though the Western territories were often in dispute, the sun moved from east to west and belonged to everyone.

CRYPTANALYST'S CHAMBER IV

QUIZ I

Words from your secret lover's billet-doux may be among these "agony-column" excerpts. With the key word, *heart,* make your own square like that in the Wheatstone/Playfair example while you remember—all's "fair" in love . . . (Answers on page 259.)

1. KR AH RH HE AW DE CR

2. OR AW MO DA HE TA RH

3. VS ST ZU DK AW LI PV QY

4. HM CA BP ZU HT ZY QD KT

5. PO AY UR QI TK BV ST QY

6. HM PM HE AW HT RY AZ

7. LK QY QY PR DQ AC

8. HA QA NA DQ AW OM BT QY

9. WR QY SR IQ WH

10. IK BT AZ CA MK BT AZ

QUIZ 2

A furious battle is raging nearby. Two brave observers have used their field glasses to see these number groups sent by your allies through the pall of artillery smoke. Can you interpret their meaning with Myer's numbers? (Answers on page 259.)

1.   221, 322, 221, 132, 111   3

2.   133, 331, 223, 223, 313, 332   3

3.   112, 331, 221   3

4.   132, 223, 222, 213, 322, 123   3

5.   322, 223, 311   33

6.   133, 312, 221, 213, 331   3

7.   331, 213, 123, 312, 133   3

8.   122, 231, 112, 322, 323   3

9.   112, 313, 313, 221, 112, 331, 332   3

10.   311, 221, 112, 323   333

QUIZ 3

The observers have suddenly been wounded. Another message has begun. You have to use your own field glasses to see the signals. Darkness is closing over the conflict, and the enemy is threatening to encircle your fellow troops. Either victory or defeat will hinge upon your skills. (Answers on page 259.)

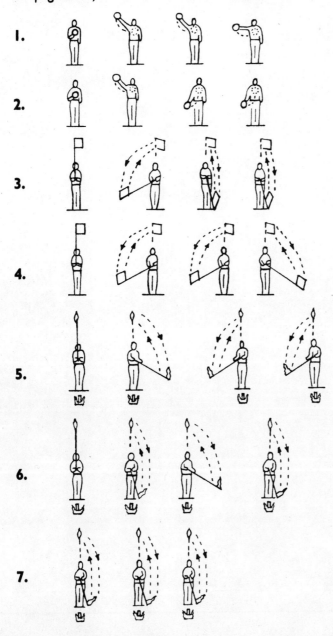

1.

2.

3.

4.

5.

6.

7.

QUIZ 4

This secret list of weapons and supplies must be conveyed rapidly by wigwag to the next observation post. You are in charge of the signal corps. Send this message with Myer's alphabet. (Answers on page 260.)

1.   cannon

2.   rifles

3.   mortars

4.   bullets

5.   powder

6.   bayonets

7.   hardtack

8.   flour

9.   salt

10.   medicine

QUIZ 5

Apply what you have learned about the transposition method called *rail fence* to discern these letter groups. (Answers on page 260.)

1. FRSM   ESAT   OTUT   RTRX

2. PNNU   ACMA   GXEI   SLRA   PINX

3. IOCA   SATE   RNLD   BTLX

4. SIOC   UCHL   HHRH

5. ATEA   CEKX   NITM   REXX

6. UINL   CAEX   NOBO   KDXX

7. CACL   OSIL   FLSX   HNEL   RVLE   ALXX

8. VCSU   GIGX   IKBR   SEEX

9. CVLY   HREX   AARC   AGSX

10. ALNA   UNDX   TATB   REXX

QUIZ 6

Reverse the cipher-solving process. Use the rail-fence method to conceal the names of these figures from the Civil War. (Answers on page 260.)

1.   Clara Barton

2.   Braxton Bragg

3.   John Brown

4.   Jubal Early

5.   Horace Greeley

6.   John Hood

7.   Julia Howe

8.   Mary Lincoln

9.   William Seward

10. Harriet Stowe

QUIZ 7

These pictographs each contain ideas relating man with the natural world. To learn more, consult the section of chapter 15 in which they are defined. (Answers on page 261.)

1.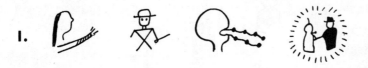

2.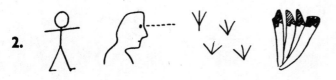

3.

4.

5.

6.

7.

8.

9.

10.

QUIZ 8

Sign language linked many Indian tribes. Consult the signs in chapter 15 to define these examples. (Answers on page 261.)

1.

2.

3.

4.

5.

6.

7.

8.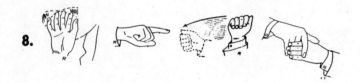

9.

10.

QUIZ 9

These heliograph signals are defined as long flash (*lf*) and short flash (*sf*). Remember that the basis of the flashes is *International* Morse Code. Equate *lf* with dash and *sf* with dot and both in turn with the correct Morse alphabet. Note: a comma separates letters and a dash separates words. (Answers on page 261.)

1. sf lf lf, sf sf, sf lf sf sf, lf sf sf—lf sf sf sf, sf sf, sf lf sf sf, sf lf sf sf—sf sf sf sf, sf sf, lf sf lf sf, lf sf lf, lf lf lf, lf sf lf

2. sf sf sf, sf sf, lf, lf, sf sf, lf sf, lf lf sf—lf sf sf sf, sf sf lf, sf lf sf sf, sf lf sf sf

3. sf lf, lf sf, lf sf, sf sf, sf—lf lf lf, sf lf, lf sf lf, sf lf sf sf, sf, lf sf lf lf

4. lf sf sf sf, sf sf lf, sf sf lf sf, sf sf lf sf, sf lf, sf lf sf sf, lf lf lf—lf sf sf sf, sf sf, sf lf sf sf, sf lf sf sf—lf sf lf sf, lf lf lf, lf sf sf, lf sf lf lf

5. lf sf lf sf, sf lf, sf lf sf sf, sf lf, lf lf, sf sf, lf, lf sf lf lf lf—sf lf lf lf, sf lf, lf sf, sf

6. sf lf lf, lf sf lf lf, sf lf, lf, lf—sf, sf lf, sf lf sf, sf lf lf sf

7. lf sf lf sf, lf lf lf, lf sf lf sf, sf sf sf sf, sf sf, sf sf sf, sf

8. lf sf sf sf, sf, sf lf sf sf, sf lf sf sf, sf—sf sf sf, lf, sf lf, sf lf sf, sf lf sf

9. lf sf lf, sf sf, lf—lf sf lf sf, sf lf, sf lf sf, sf sf sf, lf lf lf, lf sf

10. lf lf sf, sf, sf lf sf, lf lf lf, lf sf, sf sf, lf lf, lf lf lf

QUIZ 10

From a distant mesa, additional terms regarding the American West are being conveyed by heliograph. (Answers on page 261.)

1. If sf If sf, If If If, sf If If, If sf sf sf, If If If, If sf If If

2. sf If sf sf, sf If, If sf, If sf sf—If If sf, sf If sf, sf If, If sf, If

3. sf If If, sf If, If If sf, If If If, If sf—If, sf If sf, sf If, sf sf, If sf

4. sf If sf sf, If If If, If sf, If If sf—sf sf sf sf, If If If, sf If sf, If sf, sf sf sf

5. sf If sf, sf If, If sf, If If sf, sf—sf If If, sf If, sf If sf

6. If sf sf sf, sf sf If, sf sf If sf, sf sf If sf, sf If, sf If sf sf, If If If

7. sf If If, sf If, If, sf, sf If sf—sf If sf, sf sf, If If sf, sf sf sf sf, If, sf sf sf

8. sf sf sf, If If If, If sf sf—If sf sf sf, sf sf If, sf sf sf, If, sf, sf If sf

9. If sf sf sf, sf If, sf If sf, If sf sf sf, sf, If sf sf—sf If If, sf sf, sf If sf, sf

10. sf sf sf sf, If If If, If If, sf, sf sf sf, If, sf, sf If, If sf sf

V.

THE

MODERN

ERA

16

ARTIFICIAL AND ARGOT

⟨⟨⟨⟨

The nineteenth century could certainly be titled the "Inventor's Century." This period saw the foundation of the Industrial Revolution expand to support a growth of science and technology that was unprecedented. Amidst the discoveries and creative endeavors, it is not surprising that people sought to be inventive with one of their most personal and unique means of communication, namely, language. In this chapter we will review everything from slang and jargon to purposely created means of expression.

Of course, many forms of argot, dialects, and verbal rhyming patterns predate the 1800s. The word *argot,* in fact, means the special vocabularies and idioms of people in similar occupations or lifestyles. Because many such words originate among reclusive families or self-protective city dwellers, it is difficult to pinpoint the dates or locations of origin.

For example, one of the better-known forms of British dialect is Cockney, named for the people who live in London's East End. According to British tradition, people born within hearing range of the Bow Bells—so called because they belonged to the church of St. Mary-le-Bow—were Cockneys. This prominent dialect is noted for pronounced gliding from one vowel to another in the same syllable (diphthongization). In addition, the letter *r* is added to certain words, and the first *h* is dropped from others. If one were to spell some common words the way they were spoken by Cockneys, this list would be typical:

COCKNEY	ENGLISH
'arf	*half*
'cos	*because*

larf	*laugh*
marf	*mouth*
orl	*all*
pore	*poor*
wiv	*with*
wot	*what*

From the late 1700s through the 1800s, other distinct groups like pickpockets and thieves slowly but steadily created and nurtured different kinds of rhyming slang particular to their wandering and illegal activities. In many of the larger cities in the British Isles, this jargon served to conceal the true meaning of everything from comments about passersby to criminal behavior. Often these individuals just made up statements with words that rhymed with the ones they replaced. This pastime spread in popularity until it even found a niche among the country gentry for a time.

Ponder these typical phrases and try to determine their real meanings. (Remember, aural clues and similarities are important):

1. Squash the new from yer sands.
2. Go'or vest mar fer some blotch.
3. Gi' up pears fer yer tup o 'fisherman's daughter.

If you really feel stumped on the first example (and most people do when they first hear or read such phrases), try going through a group of words that sound like *squash:* for example, *gosh, josh, posh, quash, wash.* Perhaps none of these seems quite applicable yet. Then do the same thing with the word *new:* for example, *cue, ewe, few, glue, hue, mew, stew, view.* Nothing yet? Try combining some of these choices in place of the originals.

Gosh the cue from yer sands.
Posh the few from yer sands.
Quash the hue from yer sands.

Perhaps it still seems puzzling. Now look at the word *sands,* and compare words of similar sound: *bands, fans, hands, tans, lands, stands.* If you remember that the sentence contains the word *yer* (your), some of these words will fit better than others. *Your bands* and *your tans* don't make much sense. But what about *your lands* or *your stands?* Let's try some other variations:

> Josh the cue from your lands.
> Posh the view from your hands.
> Wash the hue from your hands.

This third sentence now makes much more sense, except for the word *hue.* It becomes completely sensible if we substitute either *stew* or *glue.* Depending on the situation, either might apply.

> Wash the stew from your hands.
> Wash the glue from your hands.

Having seen how you can use the alphabet and similar sounds to interpret this rhyming slang, try your hand with the other examples. The following are conceivable answers:

> 2. Go 'or vest mar fer some blotch.
> *(A) Go over to west bar for some scotch.*
>
> 3. Gi 'up pears fer yer tup o' fisherman's daughter.
> *(A) Get up the stairs for your sup (sip) of water.*

Fisherman's daughter becomes *water?* "Foul," you cry. Perhaps you're right. But then again, this slang was intentionally made difficult to comprehend. It purposely did *not* have a discernible pattern of sentence structure or pronunciation. An individual could not be certain that he could convey his meaning to an uninitiated friend. Thus, many word fanciers began to lose interest when these slang practitioners started to go to extremes in trying to vary their creations and still make them rhyme. As their popularity waned, the predominant users remained the "dips" (pickpockets), forgers, and swindlers.

Other types of spoken codes that had alternating periods of popularity in Europe during the 1800s were *Turkey Irish* and *Opish.* Both of them had origins that were vaguely traced to schooldays' games in Europe and England. Both were quite simple methods involving the addition of an extra syllable or letter pair to a word. Neither was capable (on paper) of masking any written intentions from a skilled codebreaker for very long. However, when verbalized rapidly by an experienced speaker, both tended to sound like foreign tongues, and both provided amusing verbal entertainment.

Turkey Irish added the letter pairs like *ac* before every *vowel* in a word. Thus, a word like *wary* became *wacaracy* (with *y* as a vowel). When a word had back-to-back vowels such as the word *guard*, the letter pair was placed before the first vowel to create *gacuard*. By saying these two words—*wacaracy* and *gacuard*—aloud, one can already imagine how confusing Turkey Irish could be.

Opish operated on a similar principle: the letters *o* and *p* (hence the name) were placed *after* each *consonant*. For example, the Opish version of *patrol* would be *popatopropolop*. Whether it helped cover up a meaning or not, it was certainly enjoyable to say. A person who patrols, *a sentry*, becomes a *sopenoptopropy*. A sentence containing even a few words so constructed would be quite an earful and quite difficult for an amateur eavesdropper to discern.

Altered word usages and curious phrases were found in two other invented "languages," *Pig Latin* and *Macaronics*. Pig Latin was not an adaptation of Latin. Rather, it was a purposeful alteration of English-language source words. Let's use the word *Wednesday* as an example of the principles of Pig Latin. The first consonant, or cluster of consonants, is combined with the syllable *ay* (pronounced ā). This new syllable is placed at the end of the word. The first vowel and any additional letters remain in their set position. In this case, *ednesday* combines with *W* and *ay* to form the contrived word, *ednesday-Way*. The pattern can be extended to sentences to create more audible hijinks. Do you have a "translation" for this sentence? *E-shay ill-way avel-tray efore-bay onday-may.* Just remove the "ays," place the consonants before the vowels, and you will have: *She will travel before Monday.*

The style of verbal burlesque known as Macaronics mixes vernacular words in a Latin context. The term seems to have been created in 1517 by the poet Teofilo Folengo. In that year he wrote a poem entitled "Liber Macaronices." In it he described "macaronic art," mixtures of forms and meanings. Thus, the term had come to indicate a medley of usages. By this combined style, *verbum* (Latin for word) could have an *s* appended to it, be combined with the word *they*, and thus turned into the totally contrived, *they verbums*. With a further stretch of the imagination this became *they were bums*. Because of such loosely connected links, macaronic word play didn't lend itself to verbal codes as easily as Opish or Turkey Irish.

Two other interesting languages were Chinese pidgin and Melanesian pidgin. The term *pidgin* apparently had its origins in the Chinese pronunciation of the English word *business*. In Asian ports, various Oriental languages and English traders' jargon were combined, of necessity, to facilitate trade. The same was true in the South Pacific among the Melanesian peoples and Great Britain's captains of commerce. Of course the French, Dutch, and others sailed these vast waters too. Yet for some reason English became the hybrid language for many years as a type of business code.

Chinese pidgin is familiar to many mainly because numerous writers and moviemakers have represented Oriental people using this language. But such ubiquitous words as *chop-chop* (for *hurry*) and a few others tossed in for "local" color barely do justice to these unusual hybrids, not to mention these culturally complex peoples. The Chinese version differs from the Melanesian in a number of ways, including using an *r* sound to substitute for *l;* and adding the letters *lo* or *ee* to word endings.

Melanesian pidgin developed into a vocabulary of more than one-thousand three-hundred words. It is a combination made up almost entirely of English and Melanesian, the mixture of tongues found in the Pacific from the Fiji to the Admiralty Islands. Here are some examples of Melanesian pidgin and their English equivalents:

aiting—*I think*

aratsait—*outside*

asken—*ask*

bihain—*at the rear, behind*

bikples—*mainland*

bolong (en)—*belong, of, has*

bekim tok—*replied*

boss—*leader, main man*

em—*her, it, them, they*

ewei—*away*

filimgut—*feel good*

giraun—*soil*

hariap—*hurry*

Mandei—*Monday*

Manki—*man, kid*

mi—*I*

moni—*money*

monitaim—*morning*

naispela—*nice fella*

Nara—*woman's name*

nating—*nothing*

numbawan—*number one*

ologeta—*altogether*

painam—*find*

planti—*plenty*

ples—*place*

hatpela—*hot fella*

hattaim—*hot time*

haus—*house*

hausat—*how's that?*

hia—*here*

im—*it*

insaet—*inside*

kamap—*be revealed, arrive*

kem—*come*

kwiktaim—*quick time*

laikim—*like*

lait—*light*

lam—*lamp*

long—*about, by, from, into*

longwei—*far, distant*

man—*man*

reri—*ready*

ron—*run*

rum—*room*

slip—*sleep*

spik—*speak*

stap—*stop*

tanim bek—*turn back, come back*

tasol—*but*

tok tiru—*tell truth*

tudak—*to, at dark*

tulait—*to, at daylight*

tumas—*too much*

win—*wind, gas*

wok—*work*

wokabout long—*walk around to*

yu—*you*

Now here are some sentences followed by their translations:

1. Nuspepa tok tiru.
2. Em haitim nating.
3. Aiting stima longwei.
4. Win kamap kwiktaim.

1. *Newspaper speak the truth.*
2. *They conceal nothing.*
3. *I think steamship far away.*
4. *Wind arrive quickly.*

All of the previous styles of speech developed in a more or less unstructured fashion. On a more formal basis, languages have been categorized as *international, universal,* and *artificial.* These first two names refer to languages that expanded beyond the nations or regions of their origin to become accepted and used worldwide. The third term is applied to languages that were purposely constructed in attempts to create a common one for all.

The most prominent international tongue used over many years was Latin. Though Latin is no longer actively spoken, its influence has continued from the days of the Roman Empire. It can be found in everything from Catholic Church ceremonies to medical texts. Latin remains the basis of the Romance languages, with hundreds of word roots in active use.

Other languages have become international for varied reasons. Because of India's size and large population, Hindustani has spread beyond its early boundaries to become known and used in the nations bordering India and wherever Indian people have established communities. In the 1600s French started to be accepted as the special tongue of diplomats. The influence of France in the Middle East was responsible for the creation of a form of hybrid speech in that multicultural region. This was the original lingua franca, a combination of French, Arabic, Turkish, Italian, Spanish, and Greek.

Since diplomacy, trade, and the welfare of many countries were so directly affected by difficulties in communication, people began to seek ways of circumventing or bridging these barriers. From the 1500s onward scholars have been considering what are termed *a priori* languages. By deductive reasoning, philosophers like René Descartes (1596–1650) and Wilhelm Leibnitz (1646–1716) theorized that a generalized tongue based on logic could be constructed. These two philosopher-mathematicians gave credibility to the search for an international language.

Attempts to develop a universal language have covered the gamut of the misguided, the bizarre, and the unusual. One talented musician, Jean François Sudre, created what he called *Solresol* in 1817. Its vocabulary was constructed by combining syllables as they related to tonal qualities, more specifically, the syllables that identified the notes of the musical scale. Though clever, this method was limited because it was linked to music, which is generally regarded as a source of enjoyment and not as part of a word system. Therefore, Solresol also faded into obscurity.

The proponents of international communications began to see that they needed an artificial language that was not connected to a specific nation or method, like music. Additionally, it had to have a broad vocabulary that incorporated the best elements of many well-known tongues. The first major attempt that gained a fairly wide measure of acceptance was *Volapuk.*

Volapuk (*vol,* world + *puk,* language) which translates to "world speech" was created by the German Johann Martin Schleyer in 1879. A Catholic priest in Baden, Schleyer was fascinated by world trade. His religious beliefs encouraged the brotherhood of mankind. Inspired to make a personal contribution, he applied himself to the arduous search for a universal language. Somehow his devotion and youthful vitality combined to lead him along a path others either had not taken or had not completed. He saw the journey through to its conclusion by inventing a "universal alphabet." It purportedly included the speech sounds of every major language. He compiled a vocabulary and grammar with the following principles as his foundation:

1. *Vowels*—a, e, i, o, u, ä, ö, ü (prounounced as in German)
2. *Consonants*—Most pronounced as in English.
3. *Root Words*—Mainly Latin, English, and German.
4. *Adverbs and Adjectives*—Indicated by suffixes: -ik (adj.); -o (adv.)
5. *Verbs*—A prefix indicated tense, and personal pronouns were added as suffixes.

Volapuk's popularity was like a comet. It flared brightly when first introduced to a world seemingly eager for such development, but it left the world of practical use just as rapidly. It was a victim of the all-too-human scholastic factions who wanted to decide how the future world would speak. Their divisiveness undercut chances for expansion beyond a very limited range.

The second and more stable major artificial language developed was *Esperanto*. It was created by a Polish oculist named Ludwig L. Zamenhof in 1887. Esperanto is a coined name that Zamenhof derived from the French *esperer* or the Spanish *esperar* meaning *to hope*. Based on Indo-European languages, it had the most success of its kind. This was due in part to Zamenhof's willingness to share its developmental changes with other scholars and artificial language devotees. Also, when put into verbal use, it had fewer rough spots than did its predecessor, Volapuk. Esperanto has the following foundation blocks:

1. Its alphabet consists of twenty-eight letters, each of which has only one sound.

2. Six standard accented letters exist: *c, g, h, j, s,* and *u.*

3. Stress in each word falls on the next-to-last syllable.

4. Verbs do not decline for number or person, which are indicated by an accompanying pronoun.

5. Verb endings express function or tense.

6. Nouns end in *-o,* adverbs in *-e,* and adjectives in *-a.* These endings are then attached to various roots.

Here is a list of basic Esperanto words relating to the home, family, the numbers 1 through 10, and some function words:

Nouns

English	Esperanto
family	familio
mother	patrino
father	patro
daughter	knabino
son	knabo
brother	frato
sister	fratino
parents	gepatroj
brothers/sisters	gefratroj
sons/daughters	gefiloj
boys/girls	geknaboj
child	infano
gentleman (Mr.)	sinjoro
lady (Mrs.)	sinjorino
home	domo
kitchen	kuirejo
dining room	manĝoĉambro
bedroom	dormoĉambro
room	ĉambro
garden	ĝardeno
car	aŭtomobilo

Verbs (Present Tense)

English	Esperanto
is	estas
says	diras
works	laboras
speak	parolas
responds	respondas
sits	sidas
stands	staras
eats	manĝas
goes	iras
sends	sendas
uses	uzas
writes	skribas
visits	visitas
loves	amas
thinks	pensas

Numbers

English	Esperanto
one	unu
two	du
three	tri
four	kvar
five	kvin
six	ses
seven	sep
eight	ok
nine	naŭ
ten	dek

Function Words

English	Esperanto
and	kaj
the	la
who, which	kiu
of, from	de
in	en
that (one)	tiu
how	kiel
to	al
about	pri
where	kie

17

FICTION AND FACT

⟨⟨⟨⟨

Since art mirrors life and vice versa, it is logical that ciphers and codes would eventually enter the realm of creative writing. Fiction would seem an obvious repository, particularly mysteries and spy novels. Nonfiction works, (and not just espionage or war accounts), have also contained their share of codes, ciphers, and secret languages. Among the many that might be considered, I have chosen a few examples that bridge time periods and depict a variety of methods.

Shakespeare's works would seem an obvious source for a historic progression. Yet only one aspect related to codes and ciphers plays a role in his works. That element is interception, the necessary action to secure some information for perusal. In the play *Henry V,* purloined letters are involved. Three lords are thus revealed to be plotting against the king and are summarily executed.

Actually a Frenchman preceded the Bard in applying more detailed facts of this nature in his writing. François Rabelais, humorist and satirist, was well ahead of Shakespeare in this regard. Writing during the early 1500s, Rabelais showed a full awareness of concealed messages, invisible inks, and the secret writings of alchemists and sorcerers alike. When parodying these facts, he wrote with his own brand of puns and riddles to further puzzle and entertain his readers.

Returning to England in the following century, we find one of the earliest recorded instances of a cipher being applied extensively to personal writing. The author is Samuel Pepys, who became famous after his private thoughts and records were made public. Beginning in 1660 this British civil servant kept a diary for some nine years in a type of shorthand. He also added mixtures of Greek, Latin, and another Romance language or two in order to mask some passages even more. While this shorthand/language combination was not all that unusual, the diary itself is noted as a literary classic. The means of concealment are remembered because Pepys's personal accounts of daily life are such a fine record of his times.

A number of years were to pass and the scene was to shift to another continent before writing with overtones of cryptology came to the fore. But when it did, it really caught the attention of America's readers. This was due largely to a man of many public and private mysteries, Edgar Allen Poe.

Poe had already succeeded as an author when he turned his attention to codes and ciphers. He first wrote about riddles and puzzles in magazine articles. His early name for solving them was "enigma guessing." Actually, he took credit for having this skill without ever describing his methods. He often invoked the always intriguing word, *hieroglyphics,* but that term, with its intimations of the secrets of Egypt, was certainly not practically applied. By no stretch of his or anyone's imagination was he revealing anything that involved. But Poe was a writer first and foremost. He knew how to arouse curiosity and then hold his reader's attention. It was this energetic vitality and flair for description that spread the word about his articles. Poe's readers remained loyal to him when he changed jobs and began working for a Philadelphia newspaper, *Alexander's Weekly Messenger.* There he increased his cipher-related columns.

Soon the paper was inundated with attempts to outwit Poe. This news quickly passed to other cities and eventually several states. Within months the author was establishing himself as a cipher solver par excellence. Very few people took umbrage with the fact that Poe artificially narrowed the range of possible entries: In his challenges he set certain guidelines of length and style that were within the limits of his modest skills. Nevertheless, the more solutions he published, the larger his readership and reputation grew.

The story that secured Poe's cryptanalytic fame and fostered a nationwide interest was "The Gold-Bug." This story was first published in *Graham's Magazine* in 1843, and though it actually contained flaws in cryptanalysis and concealment methods, it was a sensation. Within a few years it was adapted as a play and published in a book.

The "gold bug" was a fictitious gold beetle found by the protagonist, William Legrand. Legrand was living on Sullivan's Island near Charleston, South Carolina. He made a drawing of the "bug" for his friend, the story's narrator. It just so happened that Legrand drew the "bug" on a piece of paper that was later revealed to contain a secret message written in invisible ink. Legrand used a flame's heat to make the ink visible and found this substitution cipher:

```
5 3 ‡ ‡ † 3 0 5 ) ) 6 * ; 4 8 2 6 ) 4 ‡ .
) 4 ‡ ) ; 8 0 6 * ; 4 8 † 8 ¶ 6 0 ) ) 8 5
; I ‡ ( ; : ‡ * 8 † 8 3 ( 8 8 ) 5 * † ; 4 6
( ; 8 8 * 9 6 * ? ; 8 ) * ‡ ( ; 4 8 5 ) ; 5
* † 2 : * ‡ ( ; 4 9 5 6 * 2 ( 5 * - 4 ) 8 ¶
8 * ; 4 0 6 9 2 8 5 ) ; ) 6 † 8 ) 4 ‡ ‡ ; I
( ‡ 9 ; 4 8 0 8 1 ; 8 : 8 ‡ I ; 4 8 † 8 5
; 4 ) 4 8 5 † 5 2 8 8 0 6 * 8 I ( ‡ 9 ; 4 8
; ( 8 8 ; 4 ( ‡ ? 3 4 ; 4 8 ) 4 ‡ ; I 6 I
; : I 8 8 ; ‡ ? ;
```

From everything that you have learned thus far about cryptanalysis, what do you see that *recalls* some general *rules* for *cipher* breaking? Have you gotten a clue from the italicized *r*s? They are repeated. Remember *repeating, repetition,* and that other synonymous word? Now that you are thinking about *frequency,* what symbol, number, or punctuation mark appears most often? Here is a list of some of the numbers and figures with the number of times each is repeated on the right:

8—33		)—15	
;—26		*—13	
4—19		6—11	
‡—16		5—12	

The number 8 is first on the list. Since you know that this is a substitution, you should be looking for a frequently used letter. Did you happen to recall that collection of letters, *etaonrish? E* is the first letter on this list and was in fact the letter Poe substituted with 8, because he knew about repetition studies. Poe had Legrand do this, too. Though critics have correctly pointed out mistakes in Poe's application of such principles, readers were unperturbed. They turned the pages anxiously to learn that the cipher said:

```
''A good glass in the bishop's hostel in the
devil's seat-forty-one degrees and thirteen min-
utes-northeast and by north-main branch seventh
limb east side-shoot from the left eye of the
death's head-a bee-line from the tree through the
shot fifty feet out.''
```

Legrand followed the directions in this message (written by the pirate Captain Kidd). Without giving away the entire plot, it can be said that the "gold bug" had certain identifying marks that fit in with these directions. Legrand, his friends, and Poe's readers were quite pleased when the story's characters made a most rewarding discovery.

While scenes with heroines and heroes sailing or riding off into the sunset have always been popular, this theme of a puzzling message caught on among the public and other writers as well. Curiously, Poe did not attempt another such plot device. Though he continued to solve some submitted ciphers and codes, it was up to other novelists to carry on this new theme.

Within a few years, writers like Jules Verne and Sir Arthur Conan Doyle were applying similar techniques. Codes and ciphers were very adaptable to Verne's futuristic, even prophetic themes. Secret messages linked with criminal behavior provided angles tailor-made for Doyle's hero, Sherlock Holmes. Two such Holmes cases are especially suited to our discussion of hidden words and ways by which they are communicated. They are "The *Gloria Scott*" and "Adventure of the Dancing Men." The former is described by Holmes as being the first case in which he was ever involved.

Sadly, for readers who wanted to see a scintillating *femme fatale* enter Sherlock's world, Gloria was not a lady, (human, that is). Rather, she was a lady in seaman's terms—a ship. Holmes uncovered the tragic events linked to the *Gloria Scott* during his college days.

The father of his college friend Victor Trevor had suffered a fatal stroke after receiving a strange note. Because he had been at the Trevor's country home earlier, Holmes recognized the name *Hudson* among the words. He knew that this Hudson had seriously upset the elder Trevor before. Thus, Homes applied his mind to the task of unraveling the following message:

```
The supply of game for London is going stead-
```

```
ily up. Head keeper Hudson, we believe, has
been now told to receive all orders for fly-
paper and for preservation of your hen-pheas-
ant's life.
```

Holmes tried switching the locations of words and reading them backward. Before disclosing what he learned, it seems appropriate to let you, the reader, have a "go" at it. Before you begin, here is a clue for you: Think about Sir John Trevanion, who was discussed in chapter 4. Do you remember the means by which he learned the facts that saved his life? If you don't, either return to his story or think about the number 3. It could very well be just that. Then again, 3 can be associated with: trey, triad, treble, trilogy, third, thrice—just a minute. Did the word *third* sound familiar to you? Well, it should. It was the *third* letter after each punctuation mark that spelled the life-saving message for Trevanion. A very similar pattern was the key to Holmes's solution. Are you getting any closer? Since there are only two periods and two commas punctuating the missive in question, punctuation clearly isn't the key. But if you begin with the first word, *The,* and simply count every *third* word thereafter, you find:

```
The game is up. Hudson has told all. Fly for
your life.
```

Once this warning was understood, other written facts were discovered and Holmes achieved his initial success.

Doyle and Holmes were at it again in "Adventure of the Dancing Men." This story involved an English squire's wife who was receiving messages. These odd communications were placed on surfaces around the squire's home and written with chalk. Apparently children's scribbles, they really held intimidating meanings in forms like these:

These stick men and their varied positions were a symbol cipher apparently known to a select few. They included the squire's wife, Elsie Cubitt, and one Abe Slaney, a criminal from Chicago. Holmes applied his brilliantly deductive mind to piece together a real "catch" of a solution amidst the "red herring."

Slaney's engagement to Elsie had been ruined by his criminal leanings. After she had traveled to England, he had re-entered her life. Slaney was threatening everything she held dear with his strange chalk drawings such as the messages above, which read:

```
am here   abe slaney
come elsie
```

Holmes learned this after figuring out that the symbols were a monalphabetic substitution and deciphering them. However, the squire, Hilton Cubitt, confronted Slaney and died by gunfire before Holmes could intervene.

Though unable to prevent this sad occurrence, Holmes's keen brain did not fail him. He decided to make the stick men "dance" for him. Having broken the cipher, he knew the meaning of each figure and the fact that a flag indicated the completion of a word. He also turned Slaney's self-confidence against him. Holmes correctly surmised that Slaney believed his communications were secure. Therefore, when Holmes sent a request to him by the same method, it was made to appear to be sent by Elsie.

Here is Holmes's contrived message. Using the example above for guidance, can you solve it?

Elementary, eh? Or did you get sidetracked by that unfamiliar figure 𝍠 ? If you wanted someone to "come here a_ once," what would the missing letter most likely be? a*b*, a*j*, a*n* . . . or perhaps a*t*? Yes, that's it: a brief alphabet search makes *t* the logical and, in this case, the correct choice.

America had her own heroes who used codes to fight the forces of evil. In the 1930s one such defender of justice was a mysterious man named the Shadow. In magazine stories and on radio he uncovered wrongdoing and protected the innocent. Though exposed to nearly constant danger, he kept his identity private from everyone except the woman in his life, whom we will meet shortly.

In his quest for truth, the Shadow made use of both an analytical mind and the benefits of modern technology and science about which Sherlock Holmes could only have dreamed. Along with telephones, radios, and fast cars, the Shadow dealt with his share of codes. A Shadow novelette, *The Chain of Death,* contained this fascinating example of a *directional* code:

The extra symbols at the base of the alphabet are what gives this code a different "turn" from most: these circles direct the recipient how to hold the paper on which the other figures are written, the lines inside each circle functioning like an arrow. Thus, symbol 1 means to hold the sheet normally, top and bottom positioned as usual, and to read the message in a regular left-to-right manner. Symbol 4 directs the reader to turn the paper so that its top edge is on the left (i.e., 90 degrees counterclockwise). These extra symbols can appear before or in the middle of a line of text. Therefore, even if the "enemy" understood the principles of frequency, he or she still might consider these directional symbols to be nulls. Then even frequency would be difficult to pinpoint without knowing about the shifts.

Let's apply this directional code to two statements of fact about the hero who always wore black. Have you found the extra symbol? Is there more than one? Remember them while you discern the name of his favorite lady. Then in the next set, learn the fact that only she possessed, the Shadow's real identity!

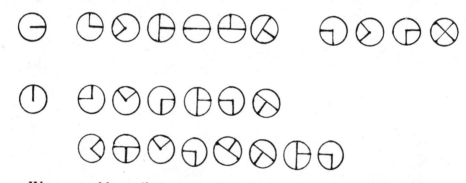

Were you able to discover the facts that were hidden in his directional code? If you were successful, you "turned" the page to the right and learned that his "number-one lady" was *Margot Lane*. The famous crime-fighter himself was *Lamont Cranston*. He was a two-fisted guy who brought crooks and enemy spies to justice come rain or shine (with the help of the beautiful and resourceful Margot, of course).

Leaving the realm of fiction, let's consider some recent practical applications of signs and symbols. One organization that is particularly renowned for its use of signs is the Boy Scouts, which was begun in 1908 by Englishman Robert Baden-Powell. By the 1930s it had expanded to become an international youth movement. Along with its sister organization, the Girl Guides (Girl Scouts in the United States), it provided many young people with beneficial instruction in such diverse fields as personal health, woodcraft, moral standards, and safety practices.

Baden-Powell's background is of interest here, as his career has an interesting link to a conflict in which the Wheatstone/Playfair Cipher was directly applied. This occurred during the controversial Boer War (1899–1902).

The British defeated the Boers, or Afrikaners, who were descendants of Dutch settlers in South Africa's Transvaal and Orange Free State. England's commanders had adapted the Wheatstone/Playfair Cipher for battlefield conditions. Its use helped with concealments and rapid transmissions of messages that led to victories.

The English also succeeded because of the individual skills of men like Baden-Powell. In military terms, he is best remembered for his brilliant defense of Mafeking, a town in the northern region of the disputed, mineral-rich territories.

By the clever use of such devices as a homemade mobile searchlight and imitation mines, and with the help of the brave young men who carried his orders by bicycle, Baden-Powell held Mafeking against Boer General Cronjé's numerically superior forces. When an English relief column finally arrived to break the siege after more than two hundred fifteen days, Baden-Powell had become a national hero in Great Britain. His creative wilderness defense methods actually enhanced his reputation as a nature expert and explorer. This in turn was a real boost to his creation of the Boy Scouts.

The full range of scouting techniques and skills is beyond the scope of this text. For our purposes, let us consider one of the direction-oriented methods: the collection of signs by which a person can leave a very helpful trail code. This method, indeed, is unsurpassed in its use of basic elements in a system providing everything from safety to lifesaving potential. The following chart depicts and identifies the various markings or caution symbols:

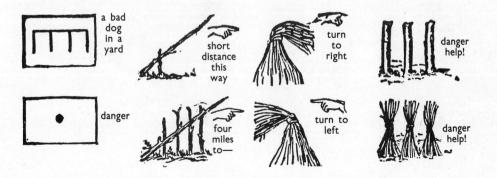

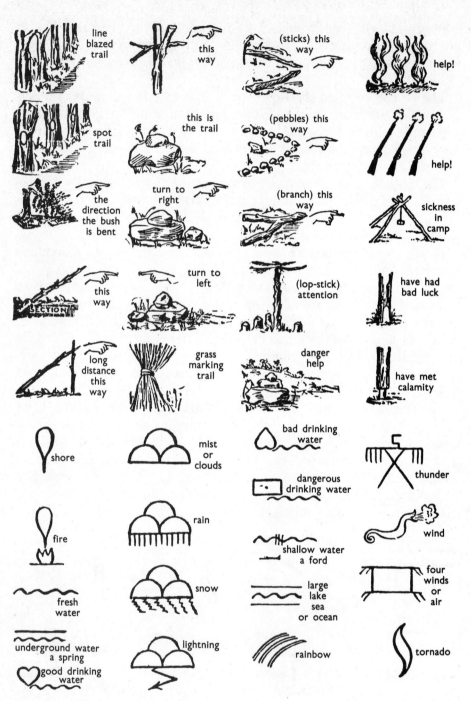

line blazed trail

this way

(sticks) this way

help!

spot trail

this is the trail

(pebbles) this way

help!

the direction the bush is bent

turn to right

(branch) this way

sickness in camp

this way

turn to left

(lop-stick) attention

have had bad luck

long distance this way

grass marking trail

danger help

have met calamity

shore

mist or clouds

bad drinking water

thunder

fire

rain

dangerous drinking water

wind

fresh water

snow

shallow water a ford

four winds or air

underground water a spring

good drinking water

lightning

large lake sea or ocean

rainbow

tornado

Each of these signs is an entity in and of itself. Now let us suppose that you found two, or even three of them at the same time. Could you follow their instructions/directions?

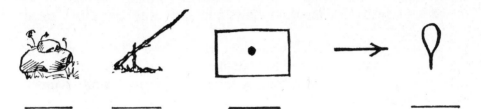

If you studied the chart, you would know that the smaller rock atop the larger one identified the path's location. But after the stick sign directed you to go a short distance, you came to a danger sign. This warning was given because smoke had been spotted. This potential sign of trouble called for caution.

Obviously, this kind of code is not meant to be concealed. Rather, its wise use has saved many lives by alerting people to anything from areas of certain danger in warfare to the hidden risks of deserts or mountain peaks. Though technology performs many wonders, you can't find CB radios and walkie-talkies growing on trees or attached to boulders. Such knowledge is always practical to have since emergencies can always be lurking around the next turn of your journey or vacation.

As can be seen by these signs, scouts are keenly aware of weather conditions. Many scouting activities, including hiking and camping, are affected by storms or temperature changes. Of course, their motto "Be prepared," means that all good scouts are ready for such occurrences.

History tells us that people have always been concerned about the elements. Among his numerous observations, Aristotle made surprisingly accurate descriptions regarding the climate of the Greek isles. While other bright men and women also contributed their ideas about such phenomena, it was not until the 1600s that truly accurate meteorological facts were gathered and compiled. This became possible because of the invention of the barometer which measures atmospheric pressure, and the thermometer, which measures temperature. These two devices enabled forecasting to leave the domain of soothsayers and rainmakers. Tea leaves and crystal balls were replaced by more accurate measurements and comparisons of such facts by seasons and then whole years.

In America, Dr. John Lining of Charleston, South Carolina, is credited with being the first man to keep diligent records concerning the forces of nature. As early as January 1738 he was interested in rainfall, temperature, and wind conditions. Eventually, Lining became so involved with this that his writing shows notations at precise times, three times a day.

Today weather is a worldwide concern, with satellites, computers and television stations devoted to both alerts and long-range predictions. With this in mind, here are some symbols that form a kind of international weather code:

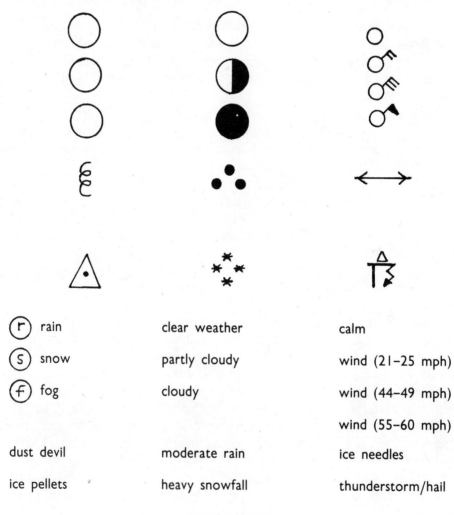

(r) rain	clear weather	calm
(s) snow	partly cloudy	wind (21–25 mph)
(f) fog	cloudy	wind (44–49 mph)
		wind (55–60 mph)
dust devil	moderate rain	ice needles
ice pellets	heavy snowfall	thunderstorm/hail

(WEATHER KEY)

18

AMERICA'S BRIEF BRILLIANCE

⊬⊬⊬

I t was to be the war to end all wars. But according to many historians, World War I ironically provided unsettled, fertile ground for the seeds of further conflict. Amidst the tragic events and the literal demise of empires, cryptology began its ascendancy.

Codes and ciphers came into prominence because of their undeniable effect on the participants in this desperate struggle. Amidst all the confusion and destruction, one particular code and one cipher profoundly altered the course of the struggle.

The code was the *Zimmerman telegram,* named for Germany's foreign minister, Arthur Zimmerman. Because of the successful naval blockade by England, Germany's resources were being depleted. Great Britain was also very dependent on the sea-lanes. Therefore, Zimmerman and others in the Kaiser's command believed that unrestricted submarine warfare could swing the balance back to the Fatherland. Yet such a broad attack would surely affect neutral shipping in general and American vessels directly. This action might bring the United States into the conflict on the allies' side.

To counteract this threat, the foreign minister suggested a political and military agreement with Mexico. Since past historic disputes and a long border existed between the United States and Mexico, this seemed like a logical idea. In exchange for an alliance with Germany, Mexico was promised territories previously lost to the United States (e.g. Texas, New Mexico, and Arizona). The German high command approved, and this proposal was sent by telegram to German diplomats with a two-part code numbered 0075.

Code 0075 was made up of ten thousand words and phrases that were numbered from 0000 to 9999. Different code books were needed by the sender and the receiver. Thus, messages using 0075 seemed to be well concealed.

But the Kaiser's men did not know about Room 40, Britain's cryptanalysis department. Commanded by Capt. William Hall, the experts in this department were using various means to intercept Germany's military messages and diplomatic missives. The Room 40 inhabitants were taking advantage of two facts in particular: The wireless was becoming popular, but it was vulnerable since anyone in range and on the correct wavelength was able to pick up messages. In addition, Germany's transatlantic cables had been cut. This had been done by the English vessel *Telconia* in August 1914.

Therefore, German coded messages for overseas had to be sent by three channels: (1) the "Swedish Roundabout," which was Sweden's Stockholm—London—Washington route; (2) Stockholm—Buenos Aires—Mexico City—Washington; and (3) America's own cable link from Berlin—Copenhagen—London to Washington.

Though it seems naive today, United States leaders such as President Wilson's confidant Edward House actually approved of the latter route. In a misguided, narrow-sighted attempt to be cordial to the Kaiser's followers, the United States was helping in her own potential demise. Fortunately, the Room 40 experts intercepted a message encoded by 0075. It was dated Berlin, January 16, 1917, and intended for Count Johann von Bernstorff, the German ambassador in the United States.

The recovered plaintext revealing the offer to Mexico was a stunning revelation. Hall and the others realized that Germany had provided them with a golden opportunity for finally persuading the United States to enter the war. America, with all of her safe industries and healthy manpower, was the allies' potential savior. Yet Hall did not want to admit that Room 40 had broken the code. Rather, he carefully planned events so that it appeared that American cryptanalysts had done it. The captain even planted criticisms of British intelligence efforts in English papers to misdirect German suspicion.

After United States leaders were given the facts and had consulted in profound dismay, a decision was made to release the Zimmerman telegram's contents to the American press. On March 1, 1917, nonaligned America was jolted by the German's audacity. Banner headlines across the nation reflected national outrage. The House voted 403 to 13 to arm merchant shipping. The Senate was more reserved in its judgments as questions of authenticity arose.

But then Zimmerman himself unleashed another thunderbolt by admitting that the cable's contents were true. His reasons for doing so have never been explained. This confession, added to the code's revelation, had profound results. Together they not only undercut the neutrality cause but also turned American public sentiment toward the allies in increasing numbers. People in Texas, the Southwest, and far West, who had not spent much time considering the Europeans' problems before, were now not only interested but enraged. Their homes and property were being secretly promised to Mexico! Politicians' senses were alerted to the rapid changes at the grassroots. On April 2 President Wilson asked Congress for a declaration of war. Congress agreed and soon the Yanks were sailing—over there.

While soldiers were being drafted, trained, and boarded on transports, the United States, British, and French navies rushed to work out their own signal systems to protect the troops. Along with the varied flag-hoist, new wireless, and standard Very methods, electricity was improving the status of another branch of communications: single- and multiple-element lights generally using the colors white, green, and red.

As the twentieth century began, numerous methods evolved that linked banners, oil lanterns, and electric lamps in various combinations. Flags were replaced at night by illuminated signals. Then hand-cranked "dynamos" were applied to provide current for the new lamps. The German Conz, French Ducretet, Italian Kasolowski, and Austrian Sellner variations all used lamps, red, white, and green cover shades, and code charts.

During the 1890s the American navy had adopted another French style, known as *Ardois*. It had undergone some changes, resulting in a system that used four double lamps. Illuminations were first set up according to the Myer wigwag system, with red = one and white = two. Later, International Morse became the standard, with red = dot and white = dash. Ardois continued to be used, in combination with the Very Light, even as better generators, onboard electricity sources, and flashing light systems became more common. The following alphabet chart is a representation of Ardois:

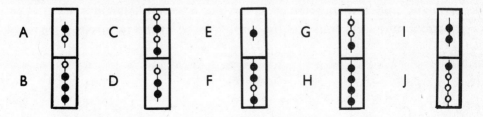

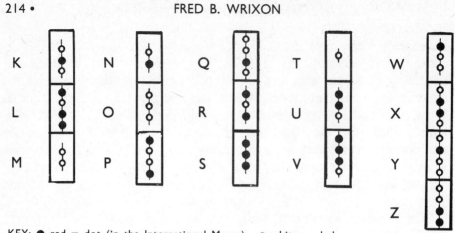

KEY: ● red = dot (in the International Morse); ○ white = dash.

The arrival of American troops in Europe, backed by the former's expansive industrial capacity, changed the course of the war. Yet it took the breaking of a major cipher to ensure that the allies would win. The credit for this achievement belonged to the French *Bureau du Chiffre* and Georges Painvin, a twenty-nine-year-old artillery captain. In peacetime Painvin had been a teacher and a musician with a latent skill for cryptanalysis. Once he was introduced to ciphers by one Captain Paulier, he demonstrated a quick aptitude for them. On March 5, 1918, a new cipher presented him with his greatest challenge. It was a system used by the archenemy of France, Kaiser Wilhelm's Germany.

This new German method was known as *ADFGX*. It was created by Col. Fritz Nebel, a contemporary of Painvin. Nebel was a skillful radio staff officer who recognized the importance of concealing radio messages. Historians generally agree that he and other officers chose the letters A, D, F, G, and X because of concern about possible jumbled airwave messages. The International Morse Code equivalents for those letters were quite distinct and helped the Germans avoid confusion.

Colonel Nebel developed a plan whereby combinations of these letters could be substituted for any plaintext. He used a square or grid method with twenty-five alphabet letters (German has no *y*). ADFGX aligned vertically and horizontally at the grid's top and left side. Then the alphabet (minus *y*) could be randomly placed in the twenty-five spaces:

	A	D	F	G	X
A	l	r	m	e	i
D	k	f	v	w	t
F	c	s	a	u	z
G	h	x	g	j	n
X	b	p	o	q	d

In the first enciphering step, the plaintext letters were substituted for paired letters. These pairs were always created by reading from the side and then the top. Thus, one pair could be AD and another FA. Using the sample grid, here is the way to arrange the order, *advance to the front at the Marne with all battalions:*

FF	XX	DF	FF	GX	FA	AG	DX	XF	DX	GA	AG
a	d	v	a	n	c	e	t	o	t	h	e

DD	AD	XF	GX	DX	FF	DX	DX	GA	AG	AF	FF	AD	GX	AG
f	r	o	n	t	a	t	t	h	e	m	a	r	n	e

DG	AX	DX	GA	FF	AA	AA	XA	FF	DX	DX	FF	AA	AX	XF	GX	FD
w	i	t	h	a	l	l	b	a	t	t	a	l	i	o	n	s

Nebel's method became even more complicated in its second stage, which involved transposition through *superenciphering,* or enciphering the cipher. The message was placed in horizontal rows across the preset number of columns (20 here). The letters were then split and placed one to a column until their total was reached (in this case 88 letters from 44 pairs). After the rows were completed, the numbers 1 to 20 were placed in random order above them. These numbers became a transposition key:

14	8	3	15	20	1	7	2	17	9	11	19	13	6	4	16	18	10	12	5
F	F	X	X	D	F	F	F	G	X	F	A	A	G	D	X	X	F	D	X
G	A	A	G	D	D	A	D	X	F	G	X	D	X	F	F	D	X	D	X
G	A	A	G	A	F	F	F	A	D	G	X	A	G	D	G	A	X	D	X
G	A	F	F	A	A	A	A	X	A	F	F	D	X	D	X	F	F	A	A
A	X	X	F	G	X	F	D												

In the third and final enciphering step, the message was written with groups of five letters. These groups were derived from the numbered columns in their original order (1 to 20). Reading vertically down line 1 produced the group FDFAX. When arriving at column 4, the process called for a fifth letter. The cipher maker simply took the first letter X of the next sequentially numbered column (5) to form DFDDX. Then, since that letter (X) had been used, column 5 began with X and picked up two of its letters, G and X, from column 6. By the time column 9 was reached, it was made up of all four letters of column 10. Column 10 was thus built from the letters of column 11 plus one from 12, and so forth. This shifting effect added to the letter groups made a very good cover, as can be seen here:

FDFAX	FDFAD	XAAFX	DFDDX	XXAGX
GXFAF	AFFAA	AXXFD	AFXXF	FGGFD
DDAAD	ADFGG	GAXGG	FFXFG	XGXAX
XDAFA	XXFDD	AAG		

The intended recipient of this cipher would have been given the substitution key, the alphabet/grid alignment for the particular message. The recipient then determined the depth of the columns by counting the total of the letters and dividing by 20. Any odd amount remaining would form an added incomplete line at the bottom, or last, row.

After filling in the vertical columns, he read the letter pairs from left to right. Then, using the substitution key, he substituted the plaintext letters for the letter pairs. This revealed the intended order.

When Captain Painvin first saw the ADFGX, it must have appeared to be an impossible visual and mental puzzle. Then, to add to his woes, the Germans added a "cipher cousin," the ADFGVX. Painvin struggled with the two over the next three and a half months. He and other French analysts strained to find any kind of clues in sources from friendly observers to intercepted German radio messages. The studies of wireless transmission locations, troop movements, ammunition requests, fuel ration lists, and the captain's strenuous efforts finally paid off at a crucial moment.

To counter the new American presence before the Yanks tipped the scales, the Kaiser's generals had planned one last major offensive. Thanks largely to Painvin's work, the spearhead of the assault was pinpointed between Compiègne and Montdidier, towns fifty miles north of Paris. The allies rushed men and materials to the region.

When the attack came on June 9, the lines of the defenders buckled but did not break. For almost a week the outcome teetered between the violent cannonades and charges of the two valiant foes. By the time the clouds of gun powder, mustard gas, and pulverized soil had settled, the German offensive had been halted. There would still be other terrible exchanges, but the direction of the war was turning because of the cipher-solving musician and the stateside soldiers who arrived in those final months of 1918.

America's star was rising sharply in world affairs. But her real cryptological brilliance resulted largely from the skills of a man who had served proudly in World War I.

Herbert O. Yardley was born on April 13, 1889. Growing up in Indiana he experienced a secure midwestern life in a golden, peaceful era of the country. He was too young to be directly involved with the only major national conflict of the time, the Spanish-American War. Yardley first became involved with the government when he began working as a code clerk in the state department.

What exciting days those must have been for a young patriot as his country's role expanded on the international stage. Being around diplomats, cables, and telegrams on a daily basis fueled Yardley's imagination with notions of adventure and intrigue. At one point he became so engrossed in trying to create a new cryptology method that he was affected by a mental malady that he self-diagnosed as "Yardley Symptom." This was a condition whereby thoughts of ciphers and codes were the last subjects on his mind at night and his first ideas upon waking.

Luckily for the world of codes and ciphers, Yardley put his "symptoms" to work to expand his knowledge and impress others. After a great deal of effort, doubtless spurred by concerns about the European conflict, he persuaded the War Department to set up a cryptology office in 1917 as a branch of Military Intelligence (MI-8).

This small but energetic group served well under Yardley's direct guidance. They dealt with such matters as German translations, invisible inks, and sabotage investigations. The MI-8 group continued to do well through the final days of the European upheavals.

Wary of a postwar letdown in cryptology, Yardley once again applied himself to the cause. He gained the confidence of Secretary of State Frank Polk. With Polk's help, enough funding was secured to begin a revised version of MI-8 in New York City. It was America's first real black chamber, set up under the auspices of the War and State departments. Soon privately called the *black chamber group,* Yardley and his staff began solving communications between embassies, businesses, and trade associations. Their work was supported by cooperative United States telegraph companies, which had national interests in mind.

In the summer of 1921 the chamber members uncovered the contents of a Japanese telegram from London to Tokyo. The subject matter concerned the possibilities for nations to meet and discuss naval policies and disputes. The people of the battle-scarred globe were known to be eager to hear about disarmament. Finding out ahead of time about such a proposal was to prove quite valuable for United States policy makers. Soon the classifications and tonnage of ships owned by various countries was to be a front-page issue.

One of the most influential meetings of nations occurred at the Washington Naval Conference in November 1921. Yardley and his associates were ready with couriers, observers, and cipher/plaintext lists. Sometimes within hours, United States officials knew the negotiating positions of Nippon and other sea powers.

Japanese ciphers revealed that their leaders would accept certain terms regarding ratios of numbers and tonnage weight of ships. If they were pressed to bargain, Japan's conference delegation was to make a series of concessions. Originally they had sought a ship ratio of 10:7. This meant that they wanted to be able to build 7 capital vessels to every 10 built by America and England. Every ratio difference of 0.5 equaled 50,000 shipping tons. Capital ships were considered to be vessels over 10,000 tons, bearing eight-inch or larger guns. In addition to their military capability, they were symbols of national prestige.

With Tokyo's secrets in mind, the United States was able to exert extra bargaining clout at just the right time. Japan's representatives had to accept a ratio of 10:6. The closing agreement, called the *Five-Power-Treaty,* included the above-mentioned nations, France, and Italy. Thanks largely to the Yardley staff, this conference ended as an important diplomatic victory for the United States.

Amazingly, just a few years after this remarkable achievement, the chamber's appropriations were sharply reduced. Then the two telegraph company giants, Postal and Western Union, began to be less cooperative for a variety of reasons. Without their full compliance, the cryptanalysts' work was obviously disrupted. But the telegraph companies were only one part of a larger problem as far as the chamber was concerned.

In the spirit of international good will that pervaded the middle and late 1920s, cryptology as well as spying were considered by many to be unsavory, immoral, even unpatriotic activities. When Herbert Hoover set a very high moral tone in his 1928 election victory, the tide began to turn rapidly away from cipher breaking. President Hoover's Secretary of State, Henry L. Stimson, dealt the chamber its most telling blow.

A well-meaning, idealistic man, Stimson was stunned to learn that anything like the black chamber was supported by the State Department. He wanted his branch of the government to be beyond reproach in its dealings with other countries. Stimson did not believe that gentlemen and diplomats should be reading mail belonging to others. With self-righteous indignation, he deliberately stopped all funding for the chamber, and it soon had to be closed.

As the first gray clouds of economic instability loomed on the financial horizon, and while the distant thunderlike rumble of Japanese artillery began to reverberate across the Chinese landscape, America's brilliant but brief cryptological efforts came to a virtual standstill.

Yardley was affected by the Wall Street Stock Market crash, yet cryptology helped him rise above it. Understandably bitter about the demise of the chamber, Yardley put his recollections together on paper in *The American Black Chamber.* This book was as surprisingly popular as it was controversial. Officials on many levels debated its merits, several issues of national policy were raised, and the public in general became fascinated, at least for a time, with the world of codes and ciphers. Then the market collapsed and most minds and hearts became fixated on the basics of daily existence. With the Depression era in mind, let us turn to consider an unusual type of secret language that became prominent in the late twenties and exists to the present day.

Because of the calamitous business climate after 1929, the loss of jobs, and the resulting social unrest, many people began moving around the country seeking work and a chance to start anew. Of course, there have always been a certain number of people, especially men, who chose the freedom of the road. With so many traveling, wandering, hitchhiking, or riding the rails in boxcars, a kind of argot began to be used for mutual benefit. These veterans of the byways expressed themselves with a spoken jargon and pictographlike drawings. By these means, they directed each other to the necessities of life: food, water, and sometimes, with luck, even a hobo's haven, a warm, dry place with a roof above and a soft spot for one's head.

To this day, this secret language and its associated pictograph symbols are maintained by a group of modern "Knights of the Road." These individuals use this title in their published newspaper and maintain a sense of pride in their lifestyle. Here are some examples of their phraseology followed by a chart of their visual signs:

HOBO TERM	DEFINITION
Apple knocker	*Hobo who picks apples*
Bad order	*Damaged boxcar*
Bindle stiff	*Man who carries his belongings in burlap sacks*
Boodle	*Variously meant: a crowd, a bribe, robbery loot*
Bulls	*Railroad policemen*
Catch back	*Return by same freight route*
Drag line hop	*To board a train when it is on a side track*
Five hundred miles	*A freight train that stopped only at rail sites 500 miles apart*
Gandy dancers	*Railroad section gang workers*
Jungle	*Camp, welcome shelter, sometimes food*
Junking	*Seeking scrap metal to sell or barter*
Homeguards	*Tramps who avoid traveling*
Hotshot	*The through-freight on a main line*
Nose divers	*Rescue-mission regulars*
Open	*Variously: friendly town or resident's home*

no alcohol	tell sad story	not kind	safe camp	unsafe place	night lodging
town awake	sick care	gentleman	don't give up	lend yourself	dishonest man
go	woman	railroad police	next, right	food for chores	stay away
danger	judge	be quiet	handout	town asleep	man with gun
kind lady	halt	alcohol	officer	sleep in hayloft	very good

(HOBO SIGN KEY)

Outside 'bo	*A Hobo who spends winters mainly outdoors*
Over the hump	*Ride over the Rocky Mountains*
Reefer	*Refrigerated rail car*
Rubber tramps	*Men who travel/dwell in old cars*
Sally	*Salvation Army, the saving factor in many hobos' lives*

As colorful as the hobos' lifestyle was in the 1930s, we must not forget that the primary cause of such mass wanderings was the Depression. The majority of these uprooted people were able to find work and thus a chance for a more secure home life because of another calamity, World War II.

19

RISING SUN, PURPLE SUNSET

←←←

Never had an inward-looking policy been so blind. This influential pre-1941 way of thinking in America was called *isolationism*. The disillusion with international events that was pervasive after World War I helped foster such a mood. Soon it became a kind of philosophy with political influence. Eventually this attitude held the country with a grip that was almost physical in its power to direct the eyes, ears, and hearts of people away from increasing signs of worldwide danger. This was true for many American citizens on the night of December 6, 1941. Yet less than twelve hours later, because of an infamous assault on a relatively unknown place called Pearl Harbor, the world, for most Americans, was turned upside-down.

The destruction of much of the Pacific fleet at this supposedly impregnable island bastion united the fifty states in a common cause. The naive times when "gentlemen" ambassadors didn't read each others' mail were gone forever. Our civilian and military leaders had been jolted with stark realizations.

The Axis countries were scheming behind embassy walls nearly as much as they were plotting tactics on the battlefield. Their spies were infiltrating our overseas bases almost as rapidly as they were demolishing defenseless villages with their howitzers. They had created technologies of warfare that made United States factories look obsolete by comparison.

Thus, in addition to the massive task of putting the economy on a wartime basis, we had an immediate need for vastly improved intelligence capabilities. No longer could we wait to respond to enemy actions. We had to have the knowledge to be able to act decisively in defense of the nation's vital interests.

America was not completely unprepared as far as cryptology was concerned. In spite of the poor treatment of Herbert Yardley and his staff, other visionary cryptologists had been quietly at work within the United States military. One of these men was Joseph Mauborgne, a member of the Army Signal Corps.

After having solved a Playfair cipher, he wrote a manual about his methods. Completed during World War I, his writing was the first such printed by the government. His contributions during the war certainly rivaled Yardley's. Mauborgne invented an unbreakable cipher, a type of one-time system. It was based on studies of the Baudot code for the teletypewriter. Its special element was a randomly chosen key, which Mauborgne defined as a series of numbers, electric pulses and spaces, or letters. The key's random qualities meant that any repetitive elements would be avoided. Also, the possible sequences would be endless. A key would be recorded for the use of the sender and recipient, but once used, it was never repeated. A list of keys for different days existed. Careful records were kept at both ends of the message transmission to avoid mistakes.

Suppose that the key was a series of numbers like 44207786358173, etc. Enciphering would begin by converting the letters of the plaintext message into numbers. Since American policy makers had serious concerns about the Pacific Ocean region in Mauborgne's time, we will use the word *Pacific* as the plaintext. For ease of explanation here, encipher as follows: $a = 01$, $b = 02$, $c = 03$, etc. Thus $p = 16$, $a = 01$, $c = 03$, $i = 09$, $f = 06$, $i = 09$, $c = 03$. Pacific is: 16010309060903. This number is placed beneath the random key mentioned above. These two numbers are added, but use *noncarrying* addition (e.g., 108 + 102 = 200):

$$44207786358173$$
$$+ \ 16010309060903$$
$$\overline{50217085318076}$$

This sum is the cryptogram. After the receiver gets it, she or he writes this number above the pre-arranged key (442077, etc.) and subtracts the latter from the former:

$$50217085318076$$
$$- \ 44207786358173$$
$$\overline{16010309060903}$$

In this step, the subtraction is done without borrowing from the column to the left (e.g., 70 − 77 = 03).

Mauborgne had achieved the cryptographer's dream of an unbreakable cipher. Its random uncertainties prevented any cryptanalyst of the day from gaining any clues. However, his discovery did not achieve widespread military and diplomatic use. Even in the 1920s there was a need for sending a number of communications in rapid succession. Because keys were inadvertently reused, and since fresh key groups were always needed, practicality superseded creativity. Nevertheless, Mauborgne's niche among honored cryptologists is secure. In addition to developing this method, he helped create the United States' Signal Intelligence Service (S.I.S.). This branch of the Signal Corps helped fill some of the vacuum caused by the closing of Yardley's black chamber.

Mauborgne's symbolic torch was passed to William Friedman, a contemporary of equal genius whose effect on our military cryptology was even more profound.

Friedman was a botany geneticist whose real interest in codes and ciphers coincided with the advancement of what can be called cryptology's "machine age." By the 1920s, discoveries in electronics and engineering had resulted in electromechanical devices that could create ciphers of increasing complexity. Friedman studied their electrical connections and keyboards and used mathematical inductive reasoning to break codes and ciphers with amazing frequency.

Working at a kind of early "think tank" called Riverbank in Geneva, Illinois, Friedman applied futuristic theories of cipher alphabet construction, frequency distribution, and statistics to the machines and their functions. He firmly linked cryptology and mathematics. His efforts led to a job with the War Department and rapid advancement to the position of chief civilian cryptanalyst of the Army Signal Corps.

Friedman, Signal Corps cipher solvers, and the American Navy Department's counterpart, called OP-20-G, had joined forces before the outbreak of hostilities with Japan. In one of the most terrible "what-if" situations in history, American cryptanalysts almost put everything together before the December 7 disaster. Here is a brief summary of those fateful events.

Throughout the late 1920s and 1930s, United States military officials had given Japan the code name Orange. Our cryptanalysts had broken one of their machine-made ciphers which was codenamed *Red*. Thus, historian David Kahn proposes that as their machine ciphers became more difficult to decipher, the color of our applied names for them darkened. Perhaps this was the reason that the newest device used by Japanese diplomats in World War II was called *Purple*.

In the land of the rising sun, Purple was titled *97-shiki O-bun In-ji-ki,* which means *Alphabetical Typewriter '97.* The number *97* came from the Japanese calendar year 2597, the equivalent of 1937. This machine consisted of two electric typewriters that were linked with a six-level, twenty-five point telephone exchange device. The telephone mechanism had stepping switches and a plugboard. These features enabled various cipher keys to be arranged. The process involved these stages: the chosen key was set; a message was entered on the keyboard of the first typewriter; it was sent through the maze of keyed switches and the plugboard. The result was an enciphered communication that was printed out by the second typewriter.

The *Alphabetical Typewriter '97* had a polyalphabetic foundation. It could encipher English letters and created substitutions numbering in the hundreds of thousands. This capability presented an immense challenge that at first seemed insurmountable. Nonetheless, Friedman and his associates applied themselves with feverish intensity.

Having previously uncovered Tokyo's naval conference codes (thanks to Yardley and company), American analysts were familiar with specific salutations and closings. Military radio stations around the Pacific constantly monitored radiotelegraph transmissions. Every possible clue was sought in even seemingly mundane communications. Frequencies and patterns slowly began to emerge.

Blanks were to be filled by such lucky breaks as Japanese cipher senders making mistakes and then repeating dispatches to make corrections. Amazingly, the American teams began to piece together the obscure permutations. In August 1940 they had their first awkward but readable solution.

This was followed by an even more awe-inspiring feat. Friedman and members of the S.I.S. actually built a crude but serviceable model that was a remarkable imitation of Purple. Soon this product of American engineering brilliance and mathematical insight was helping reproduce the most guarded Purple communications. So impressed was one Navy rear admiral that he called the process *Magic.* The nickname stuck, but this magic was not as fully appreciated nor as broadly applied as it should have been to alter history.

Magic was in operation the night of December 6, 1941. Japanese embassy dispatches were being picked up by Navy radio stations and sent on to the Navy Department in Washington D.C. By the fateful morning of December 7, thirteen parts of a Japanese government reply regarding negotiations had been deciphered. The fourteenth segment of the message was Tokyo's decision to break current negotiations with the United States by 1:00 P.M. that same day. OP-20-G and S.I.S. cryptanalysts knew this by 7:30 A.M. Washington time. It was not yet dawn in Hawaii. Most United States personnel were still sleeping peacefully at Schofield Barracks, Wheeler Field, and on Battleship Row. Yet a second sun, a red one, rose with the dawn that morning. Soon the horizon was dotted with steel birds, the winged messengers of doom.

Volumes have been written about the attack, the excuses made, and the blame often hastily placed at the time. Questions about everything from late warnings to mistaken radar sightings remain numerous. The answers continue to be confused, often speculative at best. Hindsight, the vantage point of many an armchair general and admiral, seems to reveal a pattern of misjudgment, inaction, and poor communications. But history also records that our defensive positions were stretched very thin and lacked the best military technology of that day.

One answer is certain. The American cryptanalysts of Purple did not fail. They broke every important missive necessary to validate reasons for action. After all, no Japanese message saying "attack Pearl Harbor" ever existed to decipher. Still, our cryptology staffs had done their work as quickly as the methods and governmental limitations of that time permitted.

The day of infamy swept away the isolationists' cause like the proverbial chaff before the wind. Citizens from Maine to Key West and Puget Sound to the Mexican border enlisted in record numbers. Yet the pervasive national urge for revenge was not enough to assure success in battle. Fail-safe strategies and clear directions were needed to break the links in the chain of conquest forged by the Japanese and their Axis allies.

While America's war plans were being formulated and pursued, some interesting communications and cipher/code systems were either in use or being developed. On sea, the navy had perfected systems with flashing lights, Morse Code adaptations, and a human-powered version of semaphore. The historic progression of this method, which was similar to wigwag, could fill several chapters. For our purposes, it should be understood that a number of such proposals had crossed the drawing board from the years of Claude Chappe to Albert Myer through the early 1900s. For vessel-to-vessel signals, semaphore was quite practical in daylight use:

Semaphore was widely used along with flaghoists for general messages before December 7, but because they remained in open display, means of concealment were sought with intense energy. The same kinds of efforts were applied to solving Tokyo's fleet ciphers, known as JN 25.

By mid-April 1942 cross-checked clues strongly indicated that the Imperial Navy was preparing to assault Port Moresby in New Guinea. This Pacific fortress was also a major defense point for nearby Australia. Relying on information provided by cryptanalysis, the new United States Pacific commander Adm. Chester Nimitz acted. He ordered a two-carrier task force to intercept the invaders.

From May 7 to 8, 1942, an engagement unique in military annals took place in the Coral Sea northeast of Australia. The conflict was the first naval battle in which the opposing vessels did not fire a shot at each other from their deck guns. Rather, carrier-based aircraft became the means of attack. Because both sides suffered losses, many analysts considered it a draw. Yet the imperial military strategy was thwarted there. A month later the combination of cipher breaking and bold United States initiative was to prove clearly decisive.

Intercepted messages, including those between Japanese scout planes, indicated that the strategic United States base at Midway Island was a target. The atoll was twelve hundred miles northwest of Hawaii. Nimitz and his staff had faith in the cipher solvers and made another crucial decision. A relatively small force was ordered to a location three hundred fifty miles to the northeast of Midway. When Japan's invasion squadron arrived on June 3, they were met by a terrible shock.

With one of the most surprising turnabouts in warfare, the American navy and fighter pilots inflicted severe losses on the invaders. Four of the carriers that had launched the attack on Pearl Harbor were sunk. By June 6 the would-be conquerors had to retreat. The high tide of the warlords' hopes had suddenly begun to ebb.

This reversal eventually became a tidal wave that swept toward the Japanese homeland. Thousands of allied service people gave their lives in the campaigns to free the Pacific island chains. Even more sacrifices might have been made had it not been for the very wise application of a secret language. The source of this very special tongue was the Navajo Indians.

The Navajos were a part of a tradition of native American service in each World War. During 1918 members of the Choctaw tribe helped in the transfer of orders to units by field telephone. In World War II, from the Pacific to North Africa and Europe, tribes including the Chippewa, Comanche, Menomini, and Hopi bravely served the United States. They helped win battles in both wars because our enemies could not understand their speech. The Navajos added to this success by using an oral code as well.

After months of experimentation and testing in military camps, the official list of code equivalents was set at approximately two hundred ten words. They included combinations of military lexicon, artificially created names for enemy-held sites, and an alphabet to spell extra or unusual phrases. The alphabet letters were given the names of birds, animals, and the like. The following brief examples demonstrate why the Axis powers were so completely fooled:

NAVAJO	PRONUNCIATION	MEANING
ant	woll-a-che	*letter* a
owl	nay-as-jah	*scout plane*
whale	low-tso	*battleship*

The two major European Axis partners, Germany and Italy, had their own cryptology organizations. For the purposes of this text, our focus will be directed toward the Nazis.

No other nation was more aware of the changes in warfare strategies and hardware than was the prewar Third Reich. Its planning, rearmament, and research were all quite advanced for that time. While their French rivals were spending millions of francs on the Maginot Line of forts, Hitler and his generals were preparing *blitzkrieg* (lightning war). Swift panzer divisions and their supply convoys drove around the flank of the supposedly impregnable Maginot bastions and rendered their armaments useless. While members of the French and Belgian general staff offices were having orders delivered by bicycle-riding couriers, the *Luftwaffe* was using paratroopers to capture key sites and commit sabotage well behind allied front lines. As the defenders scrambled to regroup with messages sent over downed telephone lines, the *Wehrmacht* was using a well-coordinated radio system to assist their brutal invasion. Yet, strangely, even as the Nazis sent western Europe reeling toward defeat, they failed in one crucial aspect of their technological awareness. Hitler and his staff thought that their main cipher machine was secure. In fact, its assumed concealment was actually providing England with the most vital intelligence.

The *Enigma* was the name of the mechanical marvel that the Nazis used for making ciphers. Its chief advantage over previous devices was the rotor, or wired code wheel. The rotor itself was made of a wheel of thick rubber or a similar material. Its circumference was lined with peglike contacts that made electrical connections by wire in a linkage that was not even but varied. When the rotor was put between plates connected to typewriter keys and given an electrical stimulus, new multiple alphabets began to be possible. As more involved rotor machines were developed in the 1930s, additional rotors were added to create an immense number of electrically generated possibilities. The highest levels of the Reich's chain of command realized this potential and incorporated the Enigma to protect their designs for conquest.

Not until some thirty years later did the world learn that the British had duplicated the Enigma and were reading the strategies of Hitler, Goering, and Rommel. The writings of F.W. Winterbotham and others have since revealed the perilous means by which the free West tottered on the brink of destruction while cipher answers were being slowly eked out. Thanks to brave Poles who smuggled information about Enigma's construction and wise men in England who saw the value of their facts, an operation called *Ultra* was born.

Ultra, the British name for the efforts to counteract Enigma, bore fruit during the Battle of Britain in 1940. Intercepted transmissions were studied and ciphers practiced on the model machines. With knowledge of *Luftwaffe* intentions and the crucial use of radar, England's fragile air defenses saved their nation.

The *Purple* solution was successfully applied in Europe. When Baron Oshima, Japan's ambassador in Germany, sent dispatches of top-level meetings to Tokyo, the Allies intercepted and deciphered them. They revealed such invaluable facts as Hitler's personal intentions and military plans.

Cryptanalysis, brave personnel, and superior materiel led to the sunset of Axis schemes.

20

COLD WAR, CURRENT CONFLICT

←⫝̸⫝̸⫝̸

The so-called master race had been thoroughly defeated by the Allied forces. Adolph Hitler's thousand-year Reich had lasted for twelve horror-filled years. Yet even as G.I. Joe and Russia's Ivan met at Torgau on Germany's Elbe River, a chill was frosting the outwardly smooth surface of the victorious alliance.

Past ideological differences, varied national aims, and misinterpretations at conferences such as the one at Yalta in the Crimea all led toward a breakup of the wartime west-east pact. The Americans and the Russians had met at the Elbe in April 1945. Eleven months later Winston Churchill made a speech at Westminster College in Missouri. On March 5, 1946, Churchill said, "From Stettin in the Baltic to Trieste in the Adriatic, an iron curtain has descended across the continent."

An iron curtain in the form of Soviet armies, secret police, and political organizers had indeed fallen with brutal force along the borders of Eastern Europe. The Baltic Letts, the Poles, Czechs, and Bulgarians had all helped cast off the yoke of Nazi tyranny. Within the year these peoples and those of Rumania, Albania, Hungary, and Yugoslavia faced an equally menacing aggression directed from Moscow. The agreements made about this region by Stalin and his cohorts at Yalta had been broken. In place of free elections and local autonomy were red army tanks, ideological propagandists, and thugs who intimidated the legitimate opposition. Inherent in this occupation was one of the most tragic realities of communism. Many of the same men and women who had so valiantly turned back Hitler's minions were now themselves being ordered to be the oppressors of other peoples.

In the next four years the United States responded with everything from humanitarian relief for Soviet-blockaded Berlin to the massive economic recovery called the Marshall Plan and the military alliance of NATO.

Still, the Soviets did not release their iron grip on the occupied lands. They had been able to subvert legitimate governments and threaten stability because the red army, communist propaganda apparatus, and spy networks that had fought the Nazis never left Eastern Europe. In every city their troops took from the *Wehrmacht,* cells of communists and their sympathizers were either in position or were placed to act on behalf of the Kremlin planners. These small but highly dedicated groups were often much better organized than their freedom-seeking countrymen.

During the war the Russian spy units had had much success with breaking Nazi ciphers and masking their own. They expanded this web of intrigue after the Third Reich collapsed. One of their best message disguises combined a former substitution of anti-Czarists with a type of irregular checkerboard and a key used only once. The checkerboard pattern, also called *straddling,* used ciphers of two different lengths (one or two numbers). This was set up to fool cryptanalysts as to which digits were meant to be pairs and which were single. Such a system equated digits and letters in a manageable pattern because the numbers at the side of the square were not completed from top to bottom. Since the first row of letters had no digit alignment at the side, different pairs were arranged.

By applying the key word *comrades,* here is a representation of how the straddling checkerboard looked:

	0	9	8	7	6	5	4	3	2	1
	c	o	m	r	a	d	e	s		
1	b	f	g	h	i	j	k	l	n	p
2	q	t	u	v	w	x	y	z	.	/

In this English-alphabet version, punctuation marks indicate full stop (.) and letter–number switches (/).

To this checkerboard, the variety of a once-used key was added. This improvement brought about the alignment of often-used letters with single digits. Numbers below ten were assigned to the common letters, e t a o n r i s. Digits from 80 to 99 were aligned with the lesser-used letters. This also mixed number pairs among these letters. There followed steps that involved placing these numbers and letters in a checkerboard and alternating them with digits. Though not used as frequently as in warfare, such secure ciphers helped connect Soviet espionage and political support groups all over Europe.

The stark reality of the Cold War became a daily concern for America's policy makers. Yet our strategies were based on our advanced scientific infrastructure and sole possession of the awesome power of the atom. This singular monopoly was shattered in 1949 when Russia successfully detonated her own atomic device.

With the help of stolen research provided by turncoats like nuclear physicists Klaus Fuchs and Allan Nunn May, the Soviet Union had done what had seemed impossible for a war-torn country to accomplish. United States security branches had to face a stunning reality. The long-held view of Russia as a snowbound, backward behemoth had to be sharply re-evaluated. The Kremlin was no longer an old Czarist fortress. It was a vital, formidable center of clever individuals who believed in their own police-state tactics and who sought to spread Communist doctrines around the world.

Lenin's students and practitioners attempted to do this with ever-more sophisticated spies and ciphers. By the 1950s Soviet agents were using a number of methods and tricks. An example of a highly efficient cipher system still in use today is the *one-time pad*.

This method evolved from the original paper pad used in the 1920s to tiny modern booklets made of substances such as highly flammable cellulose nitrate. Usually a series of "pages" thick, they often had red and black type that separated enciphering from deciphering key numbers. These were usually arranged in five-digit groups and sometimes varied in the number of columns and rows.

One-time pads worked because their only similarity to other such devices was that the sender and recipient had one of a pair. Each set varied from all of the others produced. Furthermore, a different cellulose page was used each time a message was exchanged. Once the sheet was used to create directions or orders, the encipherer destroyed it. The decipherer did the same once he read the contents. With more sophisticated machines turning out number combinations, the pads made cryptanalysis extremely difficult. Here is an example of how such a device is applied:

Suppose Russian naval agents wanted to convey information about the location of a main part of our defense triad to the Kremlin. They would first equate the letters of their message with numbers. For this purpose they might use alphabet/number groups in the following way: A–M = 14 to 26: N–Z = 1 to 13. The first part of the set-up for the dispatch would therefore look like this:

```
T    R    I    D    E    N    T       S    U    B    S
07   05   22   17   18   01   07      06   08   15   06

I    N         N    O    R    T    H       S    E    A
22   01        01   02   05   07   21      06   18   14
```

The next step would be to set up groups of five-digit random numbers as a key:

45678	55678	65678	75678
85678	95678	49560	59561
69562	79563	89564	99565
55578	56570	57571	58572
59573	31456	32445	33446
34447	35448	36457	37458
38459	39460	40461	41462

The third step would be to use these numbers either by columns or rows in a regular addition process. From the left, these numbers would be added to the number equivalents of the alphabet letters of the dispatch (i.e., 45678 + 07(T) = 45685). If rows were used, the communication of the observer to the Kremlin would be enumerated as shown on the following page:

T	R	I	D	E	N	T
45678	55678	65678	75678	85678	95678	49560
+ 07	+ 05	+ 22	+ 17	+ 18	+ 01	+ 07
45685	55683	65700	75695	85696	95679	49567

S	U	B	S	I	N
59561	69562	79563	89564	99565	55578
+ 06	+ 08	+ 15	+ 06	+ 22	+ 01
59567	69570	79578	89570	99587	55579

N	O	R	T	H	S	E	A
56570	57571	58572	59573	31456	32445	33446	34447
+ 01	+ 02	+ 05	+ 07	+ 21	+ 06	+ 18	+ 14
56571	57573	58577	59580	31477	32451	33464	34461

The recipient in Moscow would see these numbers, compare them to the appropriate pad sheet, subtract his pad's digits from them to derive the alphabet equivalents, and then identify the letters themselves since he would know their arrangement, too. After he knew the contents he would destroy his pad sheet and convey the facts to the appropriate authorities.

Of course, our organizations such as the CIA had been using similar devices with success. Through infrequent and uncertain thaws in the global chill, a kind of uncomfortable balance appeared to set in regarding East–West efforts to place eavesdropping devices and outflank each other on diplomatic tactics. But the "battle of the conjurers" (Churchill's description of espionage) was to have a decidedly different strategy by the 1960s.

Advances in science and industry were creating a vast array of equipment once imagined only in science fiction. The reality of jet planes, nuclear submarines, intercontinental ballistic missiles, and computers was making technology the focus of concern. America was making quantum leaps in so many areas that the Soviets and others began to fear a "facts gap" and reacted accordingly. A new era of industrial spying evolved and gave birth to a different breed of sell-out specialist, the technological traitor. Before considering some specific examples of treason, let us see how one of these advanced systems, the computer, can be applied to codes, ciphers, and secret languages.

Regarding the latter, computers have subsets of common tongues called *programming languages*. This is necessary because standard verbal usages are often ambiguous in definition and application. These languages have names such as COBOL (*CO*mmon *B*usiness *O*riented *L*anguage); FORTRAN (*FOR*mula *TRAN*slator); and PASCAL (named for Blaise Pascal, creator of the first mechanical calculating machine in 1690). Furthermore, they have vocabularies that seem to be growing by the month with terms like *access window, filemerge, interface,* and *memavail.*

Codes are used at the very first stages of programming. These can be as basic as I (inquiry), R (report), CM (credit memo), and OE (order entry). There are alphanumeric, application, and utility codes all set up for smooth functioning. In this format they are not meant to be hidden from those with knowledge of their meaning and application. Certainly, such simple letters and words can be assigned numbers or other names for protection. However, the real benefit to the secret-message maker comes in the expansive options available for creating codes and ciphers. A vast world opens up with millions of possibilities to confuse even a skilled cryptanalyst. Thus, the cipher solvers have to arm themselves with their own versions of these marvels.

By the 1960s technology was given the highest priority among the cloak-and-dagger set. America's industrial centers were assigned the special target emphasis that the KGB had once applied to the atomic Manhattan Project. One of the primary examples of such technological treason occurred in the mid-1970s with the case of "The Falcon and the Snowman."

As documented in Robert Lindsey's book of the same name, the falcon (Christopher Boyce) and the snowman (Andrew Lee) were young friends from California. They shared a mutual disillusionment with United States foreign and domestic affairs in the late 1960s. By a series of complicated personal choices and through the lax security of an aerospace company, Lee and Boyce were able to pass vital information to Soviet agents operating in southern California and Mexico City.

Boyce provided CIA satellite reconnaissance data and top-secret cipher lists. He did so through his work in a communications center at TRW, a defense contractor in Redondo Beach. This company frequently does weapons research and development projects for defense-related organizations. Boyce often used cryptographic teletype equipment with direct connections from TRW to CIA headquarters in Langley, Virginia.

Materials taken from these sources were transported in various ways by Lee and sold to the Soviets.

Amazingly, these offspring of respected families lived a strange, much-traveled existence while long avoiding discovery. It was Lee's impatience in making a Russian embassy contact that eventually led to their arrests. Convictions in 1977 and long prison sentences (Lee—life, Boyce—forty years) could not reverse the damage they had done. United States surveillance of Russian ballistic missile tests was compromised. Within a short time the Soviets were protecting their launches with much better coded telemetry signals. A new gap was opened in America's efforts to verify events in the vast Russian territories.

Through 1984 this account of traitorous friends ranked as one of the most costly American security breaches. Then in May 1985 news of a family-and-friend spy ring supplanted the Lee–Boyce affair. On May 20 retired United States Navy warrant officer John Walker was arrested by the FBI on suspicion of espionage. As spring became summer, news reports began to reveal a complex pattern of deceptions involving a family of navy men. In trials during 1985 and 1986 John Walker, his son Michael, John's brother Arthur, and family friend Jerry Whitworth were directly linked to a massive sell-out of American secrets. In John's case the spying had continued for as long as two decades on naval bases from Virginia to California. Yet though he had even brazenly carried top secrets around in a duffle bag, it took the efforts of his troubled ex-wife Barbara and daughter Laura to expose him.

This complex and tragic story also exemplifies the crucial importance of protecting encrypted technology. As a navy radioman, John Walker used a KL-47, an electronic rotor machine. The KL-47 was a modern version of the types of cylinder devices that had developed from Thomas Jefferson's day and improved upon the rotors of the World War II Enigma. This updated rotor mechanism was at the center of naval communications. The KGB wanted to break it so badly that they put some of their own best scientists to work on the mission.

According to Jack Kneece's book, *Family Treason,* and other recently published accounts, the Soviets succeeded in providing Walker with a palm-sized, battery-operated device. It was a continuity tester that revealed the wiring pattern of the KL-47's rotors. The Russians used this knowledge to re-create the circuitry, then applied computers to seek the millions of possible encryption variations. When Walker also handed them real cipher / code key lists after his tours of duty, the navy's protection methods were completely undermined.

John Walker's apostasy was bad enough. But when multiplied in the persons of his lieutenant commander brother, his son stationed on the aircraft carrier *Nimitz,* and Whitworth, a California cryptology expert, the result was catastrophic. Among just some of the systems compromised through broken ciphers, pilfered technical manuals, and the like were:

1. Top-secret strategies for our submarine and surface fleets.

2. Submarine base locations and equipment capabilities.

3. The SOSUS (Sound Surveillance System), the navy's sonar network, which uses hydrophones to track Russian subs.

4. Underwater map-making technology.

5. Facts from *Polaris, Tomahawk,* and *Harpoon* missile tests.

6. Computer data from space-sea surveillance and ways to penetrate the computers.

Had a United States–Soviet confrontation occurred before these technological traitors were discovered, Russia would have had the type of advantage once held by Britain with the 1940's knowledge of Enigma. History could have been repeated, perhaps fatally for America.

Technological treason is as great a danger as that created by the listening devices found in our new Moscow embassy. This threat is not just the stuff of adventure movies or political science fiction. The loss of expensively researched and developed military and industrial equipment robs every taxpayer of hard-earned dollars and threatens employment security. This directly jeopardizes the economic progress of the western alliance.

Every country has vital reasons for maintaining its own secure existence in an age where nuclear destruction is an electric impulse away. When codes, ciphers, and secret languages can also change in the blink of an eye, mutual understanding should be the goal of all nations.

CRYPTANALYST'S CHAMBER V

QUIZ I

Refer to the Melanesian pidgin vocabulary to translate this two-part account of a relationship between a woman named Nara and the ambitious Manki (man-kid). Remember, some words have several meanings. (Answers on page 262.)

Hatpela Manki bolong planti wok, tasol laikim tumas Nara. Nara bolong man numbawan boss bolong ples. Boss wok longwei bikples.

Manki wokabout long haus bolong boss. Manki painam Nara insaet.

"Mi laikim yu," Manki spik.

"Hausat?" Nara asken.

"Mi laikim yu. Mi filimgut long yu."

"Mi no laikim yu." Nara bekim tok.

"Hausat?"

"Yu tumas hatpela. Go ewei."

"Mi bolong plenti moni."

"Aiting planti—win."

"Mi laikim planti wok, planti moni," Manki spik, kamap moni.

Nara kwiktaim spik, "Yu tok tiru."

"Yu reri go slip rum?" Manki asken.

"No. Lait aratsait. Tanim bek Mandei tudak," Nara spik. "Mandei yu numbawan."

QUIZ 2

Continue to consult the Melanesian pidgin vocabulary as you learn what happened to Nara and Manki. (Answers on page 262.)

Mandei tudak, Manki tanim bek haus bolong boss.
"Nara?" Manki asken.
"Kem bihain haus," Nara bekim tok.
Manki walkabout long bihain haus, in lam lait painam Nara.
Nara aratsait rum planti giraun.
"Mi numbawan?" Manki asken.
"Yu naispela," Nara bekim tok.
"Mi hatpela. Tu reri slip rum?"
"I reri yu wok."
"Wok?"
"Wok insaet rum. Planti giraun."
"Mi no numbawan? No hattaim in slip rum?"
"Yu numbawan—numbawan wok man."
"Nara tok turu," a man spik. Boss kem in lam lait.
Manki no filimgut, want ronewei.

QUIZ 3

Make use of the basic Esperanto vocabulary to translate these statements and questions. (Answers on page 263.)

I.   La patrino visitas Sinjorino Aames.

2.   Tiu esta Arla Aames.

3.   La patro iras en la domo.

4.   Brad esta la frato.

5.   La fratino laboras en la ĝardeno.

6.   Kiel estas la aŭtomobile?

7.   Kiu manĝas en la kuirejo?

8.   Estas Brad Aames en la ĉambro?

9.   Kie estas la sinjoro?

10.   Kiu amas la knabino?

QUIZ 4

Use the Esperanto numbers to decode this combination of words and mathematic symbols. (Answers on page 263.)

1.   tri + ses × ok ÷ kvar =

2.   kvin − du × naŭ + tri =

3.   sep × tri − dek + unu =

4.   du + sep × tri − kvin =

5.   ok   × dek ÷ du + kvar =

6.   naŭ × tri − unu × du =

7.   tri × ses + ok − unu =

8.   dek ÷ du × sep + du =

9.   ses × naŭ ÷ du − ok =

10.   kvar + sep × tri − kvin =

QUIZ 5

Put on your coonskin cap and set your pathfinding sights to follow these trail-marking directions and warning signs. After the arrow, give the reason for the directional signs. (Answers on page 263.)

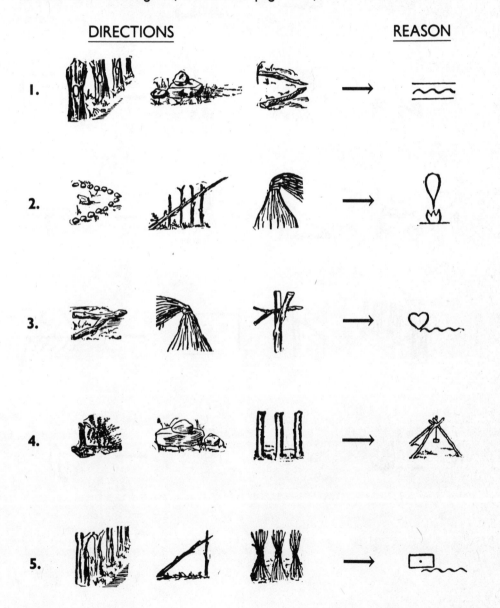

DIRECTIONS   REASON

DIRECTIONS   REASON

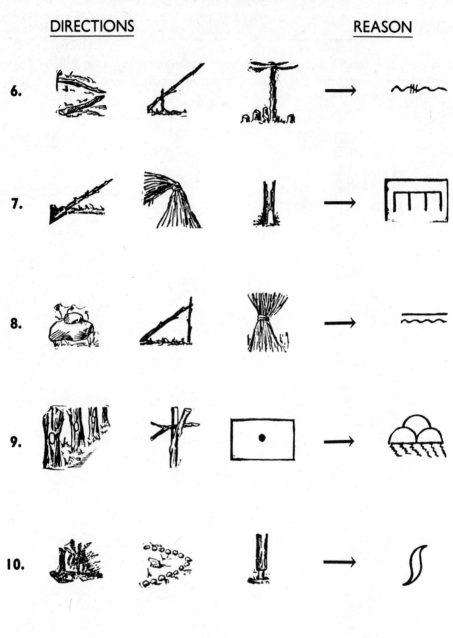

6.

7.

8.

9.

10.

QUIZ 6

Use the Ardois chart to identify these ships and aircraft from fact and fiction. Then match their names with the means of their demise or loss as listed below (A to J). (Answers on page 263.)

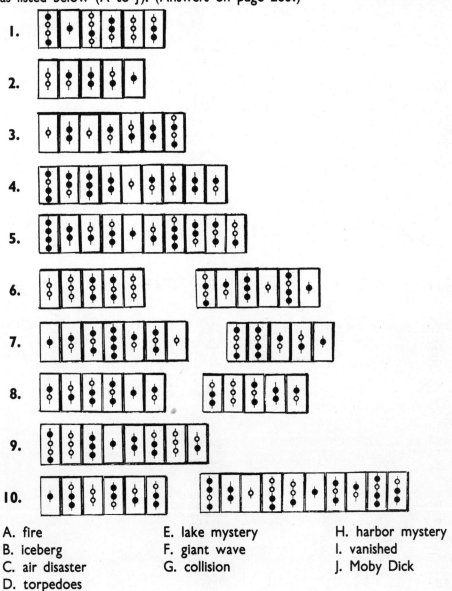

A. fire
B. iceberg
C. air disaster
D. torpedoes

E. lake mystery
F. giant wave
G. collision

H. harbor mystery
I. vanished
J. Moby Dick

QUIZ 7

If you are ever on your own, it would be wise to know the symbols for "caution," "danger," or "help" along life's highways and byways. (Answers on page 263.)

1.

2.

3.

4.

5.

6.

7.

8.

9.

10.

QUIZ 8

A brave young woman from an Asian nation has sent this terse phrase: *M = 15, alphabet sequential.* The chamber's files contain the key for her messages: *473512689036240I5789.* You have a series of ten number groups from another valid source. Use the Mauborgne system to discern the missing numbers that make the sum each time. Then match them with this particular alphabet to reveal the plaintext. You can learn that N = 16 and C = 05, etc. for your alphabet/number equations. But remember, Mauborgne's addition is different. (Answers on page 264.)

I. 47351268
  + _____
  41422762

2. 473512689036
  + _____
  574618649742

3. 4735
  + ____
  4136

4. 4735126890362401
  + _____
  4040198801312717

5. 47351268903624
  + _____
  44401661115725

6. 473512
  + _____
  523820

7. 47351268
  + _____
  67422973

8. 4735
  + ____
  5441

9. 473512689036
  + _____
  524228649337

10. 47351268903624
  + _____
  52423274014223

QUIZ 9

Recall the honored naval heroes of the world who are named in the following semaphore signals. (Answers on page 264.)

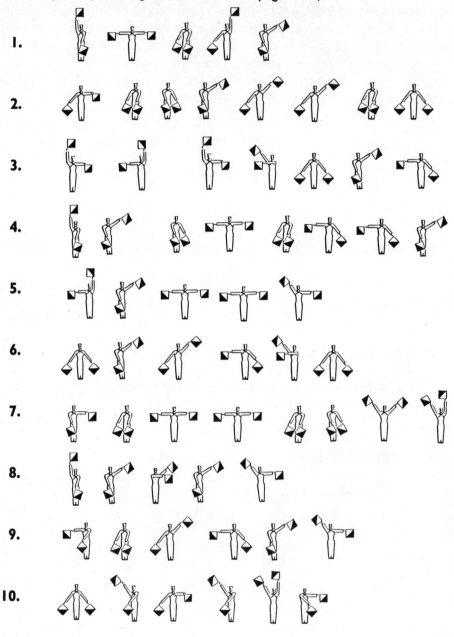

QUIZ 10

A Czech defector in Vienna has given the West vital facts from an apparently useless, crumpled piece of paper. On this KGB tear sheet are instructions for Russia's worldwide spokespersons. Add the correct column numbers (_ _ _ _ _) to the alphabet-equivalent numbers and solve their secret plans. (Answers on page 264.)

Bolshoi = 25 (standard reversed), Columns = Vertical (from top left)

54321	45678	11256
65432	56789	11267
76543	67891	11278
87654	78912	11289
98765	89123	12234
12345	91234	12245
23456	11234	12256
34567	11245	12267

+_____   +_____   +_____   +_____
54328   65458   76558   87670

+_____   +_____   +_____   +_____   +_____
98776   12367   23482   34591   45700

+_____   +_____   +_____
56801   67897   78921

+_____   +_____   +_____
89131   91257   11252

+_____   +_____   +_____   +_____   +_____
11254   11278   11293   11301   11291

ANSWERS

ANSWERS

CRYPTANALYST'S CHAMBER I

QUIZ

1.
  1. Marathon 2. Delphi 3. Athens 4. Cyclades 5. Parthenon 6. Laconia 7. Acropolis 8. Piraeus 9. Mt. Olympus 10. Peloponnesus

2.
  1. Hercules 2. Priam 3. Agamemnon 4. Laocoon 5. Helen of Troy 6. Paris 7. Achilles 8. Trojan Horse 9. Hector 10. Clytemnestra

3.
  1. Rubicon 2. Cleopatra 3. Augustus 4. Gaul 5. Brutus 6. Pompey 7. Legions 8. Antony 9. Calpurnia 10. Ides of March

4.
  1. Tribune 2. Hannibal 3. Colosseum 4. Senate 5. Huns 6. Emperor 7. Carthage 8. Attila 9. Tiber 10. Visigoths

5.
  1. cauldron 2. vial 3. beaker 4. water 5. pestle 6. scales 7. fire 8. mortar 9. lead 10. charcoal

6.
  1. Genoa 2. Constantinople 3. Venice 4. Grenada 5. Naples 6. Barcelona 7. Reims 8. Florence 9. Madrid 10. Avignon

7.
  1. Isabella 2. Polo 3. R. Bacon 4. Cortez 5. da Gama 6. Ferdinand 7. de Leon 8. Cervantes 9. Magellan 10. C. (Catherine) de Medici

8.
  1. Cape Horn 2. astrolabe 3. cartographer 4. shoreline 5. Asia passage 6. compass 7. St. Christopher 8. navigator 9. tides 10. Cape of Good Hope

9.
  1. savings 2. loan 3. demand 4. free trade 5. merchant 6. bonds 7. profit 8. investor 9. financial 10. middle class

10.
  1. witch 2. demons 3. pentacle 4. sorcery 5. evil eye 6. warlock 7. amulet 8. hex 9. potion 10. black magic

CRYPTANALYST'S CHAMBER II

QUIZ

1. **1.** Chartley Castle **2.** Walsingham **3.** Babington Plot **4.** Phelippes **5.** Ballard **6.** Scotland **7.** Philip of Spain **8.** Elizabeth **9.** Gifford **10.** Fotheringhay Castle

2. key in wall crevice

3. cellar well swim to freedom

4. **1.** 5—2 **2.** 3—6 **3.** 1—5 **4.** 5—4 **5.** 3—5 **6.** 2—2 **7.** 5—5 **8.** 1—4 **9.** 3—3 **10.** 4—4

5. **1.** Socrates **2.** Confucius **3.** Galileo **4.** Locke **5.** Buddha **6.** Nostradamus **7.** Solomon **8.** Rousseau **9.** Newton **10.** Kant

6. **1.** Plato **2.** Copernicus **3.** Mohammed **4.** Knox **5.** Aristotle **6.** St. Thomas **7.** Mendel **8.** Calvin **9.** Harvey **10.** St. Francis

7. **1.** First V.P.—J. Adams **2.** Doctrine—Monroe **3.** Mount Vernon—Washington **4.** inventor—Jefferson **5.** wife—Dolly Madison **6.** New Orleans—Jackson **7.** grandson—B. Harrison **8.** Rough and Ready—Z. Taylor **9.** bachelor—Buchanan **10.** thirteenth—Fillmore

8. **1.** honest—A. Lincoln **2.** Rough Riders—T. Roosevelt **3.** silent—Coolidge **4.** impeachment—A. Johnson **5.** Civil War hero—Grant **6.** disputed vote—Hayes **7.** son of president—J.Q. Adams **8.** terms split—Cleveland **9.** Supreme Court—Taft **10.** dark horse—J. Polk

9. **1.** faith **2.** trust **3.** charity **4.** love **5.** mercy **6.** hope **7.** peace **8.** honor **9.** truth **10.** loyalty

10. **1.** 33 **2.** 21 **3.** 29 **4.** 53 **5.** 39 **6.** 48 **7.** 15 **8.** 31 **9.** 45 **10.** 24

CRYPTANALYST'S CHAMBER III

QUIZ

1. Culper-Tallmadge alphabet chart with number equivalents

a	b	c	d	e	f	g	h	i	j	k	l	m
1,	2,	3,	4,	5,	6,	7,	8,	9,	10,	11,	12,	13
5,	6,	7,	8,	9,	10,	1,	2,	3,	4,	15,	13,	14
e	f	g	h	i	j	a	b	c	d	o	m	n

n	o	p	q	r	s	t	u	v	w	x	y	z
14,	15,	16,	17,	18,	19,	20,	21,	22,	23,	24,	25,	26
16,	17,	18,	11,	12,	21,	22,	23,	24,	25,	26,	19,	20
p	q	r	k	l	u	v	w	x	y	z	s	t

Note: Some letter/number equivalents have the same total. Continue to seek the letters needed for a correct answer. As shown here, the letters' number equivalents have been *added.*

m	r	s
13	18	19
14	12	21
n	l	u
27	30	40

1. **1.** Mrs. Washington **2.** H. Knox **3.** Revere **4.** S. Adams **5.** Von Steuben **6.** L. Darragh **7.** Franklin **8.** Rochambeau **9.** N. Hale **10.** M. (Molly) Pitcher

2. **1.** secret ink **2.** dagger **3.** trap door **4.** lamp sign **5.** go between **6.** poison **7.** hidden pocket **8.** long glass **9.** wax seal **10.** hollow bullet

3. **1.** Pinta **2.** Mayflower **3.** Half Moon **4.** Monitor **5.** Merrimac **6.** Arizona **7.** Wasp **8.** Nautilus **9.** Calypso **10.** Polaris

4. 1. I long for you. **2.** Shadows have many eyes. **3.** Beware the east gatekeeper. **4.** Servants hear too well. **5.** Watch for the lamp. **6.** Use the first corridor. **7.** Then take second staircase. **8.** Soon we will be together. **9.** Cares will vanish in my embrace. **10.** Adieu until our rendezvous.

5. Jefferson's home—Monticello; land deal—Louisiana Purchase
   1 3   10   4   9
1. 7 × 11 = 77; **2.** 17 − 4 = 13; **3.** 5 + 21 = 26; **4.** 20 ÷ 4 = 5; **5.** 24 × 7 = 168; **6.** 21 − 3 = 18; **7.** 17 × 16 = 272; **8.** 23 + 25 = 48; **9.** 18 ÷ 3 = 6; **10.** 22 × 21 = 462

6. 1. Corsica **2.** Borodino **3.** Moscow **4.** Leipzig **5.** Elba **6.** Old Guard **7.** Belgium **8.** Wellington **9.** Waterloo **10.** St. Helena

7. 1. plane crash **2.** dam break **3.** prison riot **4.** flood watch **5.** cyclone **6.** toxic fumes **7.** blizzard **8.** forest fire **9.** oil spill **10.** ptomaine

8. *Example solution for #1:*
Braille dots read a to f; letters between are b, c, d, e. Their number equivalents total 14; + Braille dots read v to z; letters between are w, x, y, whose number equivalents total 72. Thus, 14 + 72 = 86.
1. a to f (14) + v to z (72) = 86; **2.** g to k (27) − a to e (9) = 18; **3.** q to u (57) × b to d (3) = 171; **4.** l to p (42) + s to y (110) = 152; **5.** c to i (30) ÷ a to d (5) = 6; **6.** m to r (62) − h to k (19) = 43; **7.** u to x (45) × b to e (7) = 315; **8.** i to o (60) ÷ a to c (2) = 30; **9.** n to t (85) − w to y (24) = 61; **10.** e to j (30) × g to i (8) = 240

9. 1. Antares **2.** Carina **3.** Draco **4.** Hydrus **5.** Lyra **6.** Orion **7.** Perseus **8.** Serpens **9.** Tucana **10.** Vega

10. 1. Milky Way **2.** orbit **3.** light year **4.** galaxy **5.** meteors **6.** axis **7.** comet **8.** gravity **9.** asteroids **10.** North Star

CRYPTANALYST'S CHAMBER IV

QUIZ

1. *Note:* x is used as a null to make pairs in digraph stage.

1. KR AH RH HE AW DE CR	**2.** OR AW MO DA HE TA RH
(diagraph) me et at th ex ca fe	sh ex is ax th re at
(answer) Meet at the cafe.	She is a threat.
3. VS ST ZU DK AW LI PV QY	**4.** HM CA BP ZU HT ZY QD KT
yo ur un cl ex kn ow sx	ri de co un tr yx la ne
Your uncle knows.	Ride country lane.
5. PO AY UR QI TK BV ST QY	**6.** HM PM HE AW HT RY AZ
ou rx st ol en ho ur sx	ri sk th ex tr ys tx
Our stolen hours.	Risk the tryst.
7. LK QY QY PR DQ AC	**8.** HA QA NA DQ AW OM BT QY
ki sx sx se al ed	te lx lt al ex si gh sx
Kiss sealed.	Telltale sighs.
9. WR QY SR IQ WH	**10.** IK BT AZ CA MK BT AZ
ye sx my lo ve	ni gh tx de li gh tx
Yes my love.	Night delight.

2. *Note:* 3, 33, and 333 indicate *end of word, end of sentence,* and *end of message,* respectively.

    1. enemy **2.** troops **3.** are **4.** moving **5.** now **6.** their **7.** right **8.** flank **9.** appears **10.** weak
    Message: Enemy troops are moving now. Their right flank appears weak.

3.

	POSITION	MOTION			MESSAGE
1.	1	1	1	2	A
2.	1	1	3	3	T
3.	1	1	3	3	T
4.	1	1	1	2	A
5.	1	2	1	1	C
6.	1	3	2	3	K
7.		3	3	3	End of message

4. **1.** 211, 112, 322, 322, 223, 322; **2.** 331, 213, 122, 231, 221, 332; **3.** 132, 223, 331, 133, 112, 331, 332; **4.** 121, 233, 231, 231, 221, 133, 332; **5.** 313, 223, 311, 212, 221, 331; **6.** 121, 112, 111, 223, 322, 221, 133, 332; **7.** 312, 112, 331, 212, 133, 112, 211, 323; **8.** 122, 231, 223, 233, 331; **9.** 332, 112, 231, 133; **10.** 132, 221, 212, 213, 211, 213, 322, 221.   333

5. a. Divide cipher into equal halves:
  FRSM ESAT|OTUT RTRX

  b. Start with first letter on left (f), then first letter on right side of line (o) and continue alternating left to right across the dividing line. X is a null.

  1. FORT SUMTER START **2.** PENINSULAR CAMPAIGN **3.** IRON-CLADS BATTLE **4.** SHILOH CHURCH **5.** ANTIETAM CREEK **6.** UNION BLOCKADE **7.** CHANCELLORSVILLE FALLS **8.** VICKS-BURG SIEGE **9.** CAVALRY CHARGES **10.** ATLANTA BURNED

6. **1.** C A A A T N
     L R B R O X

CAAATNLRBROX

CAAA TNLR BROX

2. B A T N R G
    R X O B A G

BATNRGRXOBAG

BATN RGRX OBAG

3. J H B O N X
    O N R W X X

JHBONXONRWXX

JHBO NXON RWXX

4. J B L A L X
    U A E R Y X

JBLALXUAERYX

JBLA LXUA ERYX

5. H R C G E L Y X
    O A E R E E X X

HRCGELYXOAEREEXX

HRCG ELYX OAER EEXX

6. J H H O
    O N O D

JHHOONOD

JHHO ONOD

7. J L A O E X
    U I H W X X

JLAOEXUIHWXX

JLAO EXUI HWXX

8. M R L N O N
    A Y I C L X

MRLNONAYICLX

MRLN ONAY ICLX

9. W L I M E A D X
    I L A S W R X X

WLIMEADXILASWRXX

WLIM EADX ILAS WRXX

10. H R I T T W
    A R E S O E

HRITTWARESOE

HRIT TWAR ESOE

7.
1. Cheyenne—soldier—talk (intense)—council (A Cheyenne and a soldier talk intensely in a council.)
2. man—see—bird tracks—eagle tail (A man sees bird tracks and an eagle's tail feathers.)
3. Mandan—walk—canyon—road (A Mandan walks a canyon road.)
4. Sioux—strong—hunt—buffalo (A strong Sioux hunts a buffalo.)
5. man disabled—woman—prayer—spirits above (A man is disabled and a woman prays to the spirits above.)
6. girl—see—deer tracks—black deer (A girl sees the tracks of a black deer.)
7. medicine man—long hair—talk together—calling for rain (A medicine man and a long hair talk together and call for rain.)
8. boy—hear—wind—singing (A boy hears the wind singing.)
9. white man—wise man—call for—making peace (A white man is wise when he calls for making peace.)
10. man on horse back—see—deep snow—mountain (A man on horseback sees deep snow on the mountain.)

8.
1. I make fire (I build a fire.)
2. question you possession house (Where is your home?)
3. long time see no (I have not seen you for a long time.)
4. I go house (I am going home.)
5. question you sit (Where do you live?)
6. you arise teepee (You set up a tent.)
7. I recover ring (I recover the ring.)
8. question you possession horse (Where is your horse?)
9. I make camp (I am going to make camp.)
10. question you call (What is your name?)

9.
1. Wild Bill Hickok 2. Sitting Bull 3. Annie Oakley 4. Buffalo Bill Cody 5. Calamity Jane 6. Wyatt Earp 7. Cochise 8. Belle Starr 9. Kit Carson 10. Geronimo

10.
1. cowboy 2. land grant 3. wagon train 4. long horns 5. range war 6. buffalo 7. water rights 8. sod buster 9. barbed wire 10. homestead

CRYPTANALYST'S CHAMBER V

QUIZ

1.   Hot fella Manki has plenty of work, but he likes Nara too much. Nara belongs to the number one boss of the place. The boss works far away on the mainland.

Manki walks around to the house of the boss. Manki finds Nara inside.

"I like you," Manki speaks.

"How's that?" Nara asks.

"I like you. I feel good about you."

"I don't like you," Nara replies.

"How's that?"

"You too much hotfella. Go away."

"I have plenty money."

"I think plenty—wind."

"I like plenty work, plenty money," Manki speaks, reveals money. Nara quickly speaks, "You tell the truth."

"You ready go to sleep room?" Manki asks.

"No. Light outside. Come back Monday at dark," Nara speaks. "Monday you number one."

2.   Monday at dark, Manki comes back to the house that belongs to the boss.

"Nara?" Manki asks.

"Come behind the house," Nara replies.

Manki walks around behind the house, in the lamplight he finds Nara.

Nara is outside a room with plenty soil.

"Me number one?" Manki asks.

"You nice fella," Nara replies.

"Me hotfella. You ready for the sleep room?"

"I ready you work."

"Work?"

"Work inside room. Plenty soil."

"Me not number one? No hot time in the sleep room?"

"You number one—number one work man."

"Nara tells the truth," a man speaks. Boss comes into the lamp light.

Manki does not feel good, wants to run away.

3. **1.** The mother visits Mrs. Aames. **2.** That one is Arla Aames. **3.** The father goes in the house. **4.** Brad is the brother. **5.** The sister works in the garden. **6.** How is the car? **7.** Who eats in the kitchen? **8.** Is Brad Aames in the room? **9.** Where is the gentleman? **10.** Who loves the daughter?

4.
1. $3 + 6 \times 8 \div 4 = 18$
2. $5 - 2 \times 9 + 3 = 30$
3. $7 \times 3 - 10 + 1 = 12$
4. $2 + 7 \times 3 - 5 = 22$
5. $8 \times 10 \div 2 + 4 = 44$
6. $9 \times 3 - 1 \times 2 = 52$
7. $3 \times 6 + 8 - 1 = 25$
8. $10 \div 2 \times 7 + 2 = 37$
9. $6 \times 9 \div 2 - 8 = 19$
10. $4 + 7 \times 3 - 5 = 28$

5.
1. spot trail, turn to left, this way—reason:large lake
2. this way, four miles to, turn right—reason:fire
3. this way, turn left, this way—reason:good water
4. the bush is bent, turn right, danger help!—reason:sickness in camp
5. line blazed trail, long distance this way, danger help!—reason:dangerous water
6. this way, short distance this way, attention!—reason:a ford
7. this way, turn left, have had bad luck—reason:bad dog in yard
8. this is the trail, long distance this way, grass marking trail—reason:underground spring
9. spot trail, this way, danger—reason:snow
10. direction the bush is bent, this way, have met calamity—reason:tornado

6. **1.** Pequod—J **2.** Maine—H **3.** Titanic—B **4.** Lusitania—D **5.** Hindenburg—C **6.** Morro Castle—A **7.** Earhart plane—I **8.** Andrea Doria—G **9.** Poseidon—F **10.** Edmund Fitzgerald—E

7. **1.** town awake—officer—be quiet—go **2.** don't give up—kind lady—tell sad story—handout **3.** danger—man with gun—be quiet—go **4.** no alcohol—don't give up—tell sad story—food for chores **5.** town awake—sick care—go—woman **6.** next right—safe camp—lend yourself—handout **7.** halt—judge—dishonest man—stay away **8.** woman—very good—night lodging—town asleep **9.** danger—stay away—unsafe place—railroad police **10.** no alcohol—go—next right—sleep in hayloft

8. (Mauborgne's "difference" is noncarrying addition.)

    1.   47351268

        +04171504 bomb **2.** +101106060716 hidden **3.** +0401 by

        <u>41422762</u>

4. +03150720110503l6 American **5.** +07150403212101 Embassy

6. +150318 map **7.** +20171715 room **8.** +1716 on

9. +151716060301 Monday **10.** +15172016111609 morning

9. **1.** Drake **2.** Magellan **3.** J.P. Jones **4.** de Grasse **5.** Perry **6.** Nelson **7.** Farragut **8.** Dewey **9.** Halsey **10.** Nimitz

10. (*Note:* standard reversed means Z=1, Y=2, X=3, etc.)

54321	65432	76543	87654
+ 07 = t	+ 26 = a	+ 15 = l	+ 16 = k

98765	12345	23456	34567	45678
+ 11 = p	+ 22 = e	+ 26 = a	+ 24 = c	+ 22 = e

56789	67891	78912
+ 12 = o	+ 06 = u	+ 09 = r

89123	91234	11234
+ 08 = s	+ 23 = d	+ 18 = i

11245	11256	11267	11278	11289
+ 09 = r	+ 22 = e	+ 26 = a	+ 23 = d	+ 02 = y

talk peace our s d i ready

BIBLIOGRAPHY

Bakeless, John. *Turncoats, Traitors and Heroes.* Philadelphia: J.B. Lippincott Company, 1959.

Basham, A.L. *The Wonder That Was India.* New York: Grove Press, 1959.

Bearden, Bill, ed. *The Bluejacket's Manual,* 20th ed. Annapolis: U.S. Naval Institute, 1978.

Bittner, William. *Poe: A Biography.* Boston: Little, Brown & Co., 1962.

Boy Scouts of America. *Boy Scouts Handbook.* Irving, Texas: Boy Scouts of America, 1940.

Burton, Sir Richard. *Kāma-sūtra.* New York: E.P. Dutton & Co., 1962.

Catton, Bruce. *Glory Road.* New York: Doubleday & Co., 1952.

Cresswell, John. *Teach Yourself Esperanto.* New York: David McKay Co., 1968.

Donovan, Robert J. *Tumultuous Years.* New York: W.W. Norton & Co., 1982.

Doyle, Arthur Conan. *A Treasury of Sherlock Holmes.* New York: Hanover House, 1955.

Encyclopedia Americana, s.v. "Cyrillic Alphabet," Diringer, David.
_____, s.v. "Deafness," Doctor, Powrie V.

Folliot, Denise. *Marie Antoinette.* New York: Harper & Row, 1957.

Gould, Robert. *The History of Freemasonry Throughout the World.* New York: Charles Scribner, 1936.

Hoehling, A.A. *Women Who Spied.* New York: Dodd, Mead & Co., 1967.

Ind, Allison. *A Short History of Espionage.* New York: David McKay, 1963.

Laffin, John. *Codes and Ciphers.* New York: Abelard-Schuman, 1964.

Lewis, Spencer. *Rosicrucian.* San José: The Rosicrucian Press Ltd., 1929.

Mead, Hilary. "Captain Frederick Marryat, Royal Navy." In *Proceedings of the United States Naval Institute.* Annapolis: U.S. Naval Institute, 1933.

_____. "The History of the International Code." In *Proceedings* Annapolis: U.S. Naval Institute, 1934.

Moore, Dan. *Cloak & Cipher*. Indianapolis: The Bobbs-Merrill Co. Inc., 1962.

Murphy, John. *Book of Pidgin English*. New York: AMS Press, Inc., 1949.

Myer, Albert. *Manual of Signals*. Washington, D.C.: U.S. Government Printing Office, 1879.

"Cipher Mummery Exhumed by the *New York Tribune,*" Nast, Thomas. *Harper's Weekly,* 1878.

Niblack, A.P. "Proposed Day, Night and Fog Signals for the Navy with Brief Description of the Ardois Night System." In *Proceedings of the United States Naval Institute*. Annapolis: U.S. Naval Institute, 1891.

Peckham, Howard H. "British Secret Writing in the Revolution." *Quarterly Review of the Michigan Alumnus* 44 (Winter 1938): 126–31.

Pei, Mario. *One Language for the World*. New York: The Devin-Adair Co., 1958.

Pennypacker, Morton. *General Washington's Spies on Long Island and in New York*. Brooklyn: Long Island Historical Society, 1939.

Plaidy, Jean. *Mary Queen of Scots*. New York: G.P. Putnam, 1975.

Schachner, Nathan. *Aaron Burr: A Biography*. New York: Frederick Stokes Co., 1937.

Thorne, J.O., ed. *Chambers's Biographical Dictionary*. New York: St. Martin's Press, 1969.

Tomkins, William. *Indian Sign Language*. New York: Dover Publications, 1968.

U.S. Army Military History Institute. *Traditions of the Signal Corps*. Washington, D.C.: U.S. Government Printing Office, 1959.

Van Doren, Carl. *Secret History of the American Revolution*. New York: Viking Press, 1941.

Way, Peter. *Undercover Codes and Ciphers*. London: Aldus Books, 1977.